MATT WAGNER
WRITER

JOHN WATKISS
ARTIST, THE FACE

R.G. TAYLOR
ARTIST, THE BRUTE

DAVID HORNUNG
COLORIST

JOHN COSTANZA
LETTERER

SANDMAN MYSTERY THEATRE

THE FACE
-AND-
THE BRUTE

Karen Berger
VP-Executive Editor & Editor-original series

Shelly Roeberg
Associate Editor-original series

Scott Nybakken
Editor-collected edition

Robbin Brosterman
Senior Art Director

Amie Brockway-Metcalf
Art Director

Paul Levitz
President & Publisher

Georg Brewer
VP-Design & Retail Product Development

Richard Bruning
Senior VP-Creative Director

Patrick Caldon
Senior VP-Finance & Operations

Chris Caramalis
VP-Finance

Terri Cunningham
VP-Managing Editor

Dan DiDio
VP-Editorial

Alison Gill
VP-Manufacturing

Rich Johnson
VP-Book Trade Sales

Hank Kanalz
VP-General Manager, WildStorm

Lillian Laserson
Senior VP & General Counsel

Jim Lee
Editorial Director-WildStorm

David McKillips
VP-Advertising & Custom Publishing

John Nee
VP-Business Development

Gregory Noveck
Senior VP-Creative Affairs

Cheryl Rubin
Senior VP-Brand Management

Bob Wayne
VP-Sales & Marketing

"His people's history
was a mixture
of rage
in the name
of order, and
death
in the name of
pride."

-THE FACE-

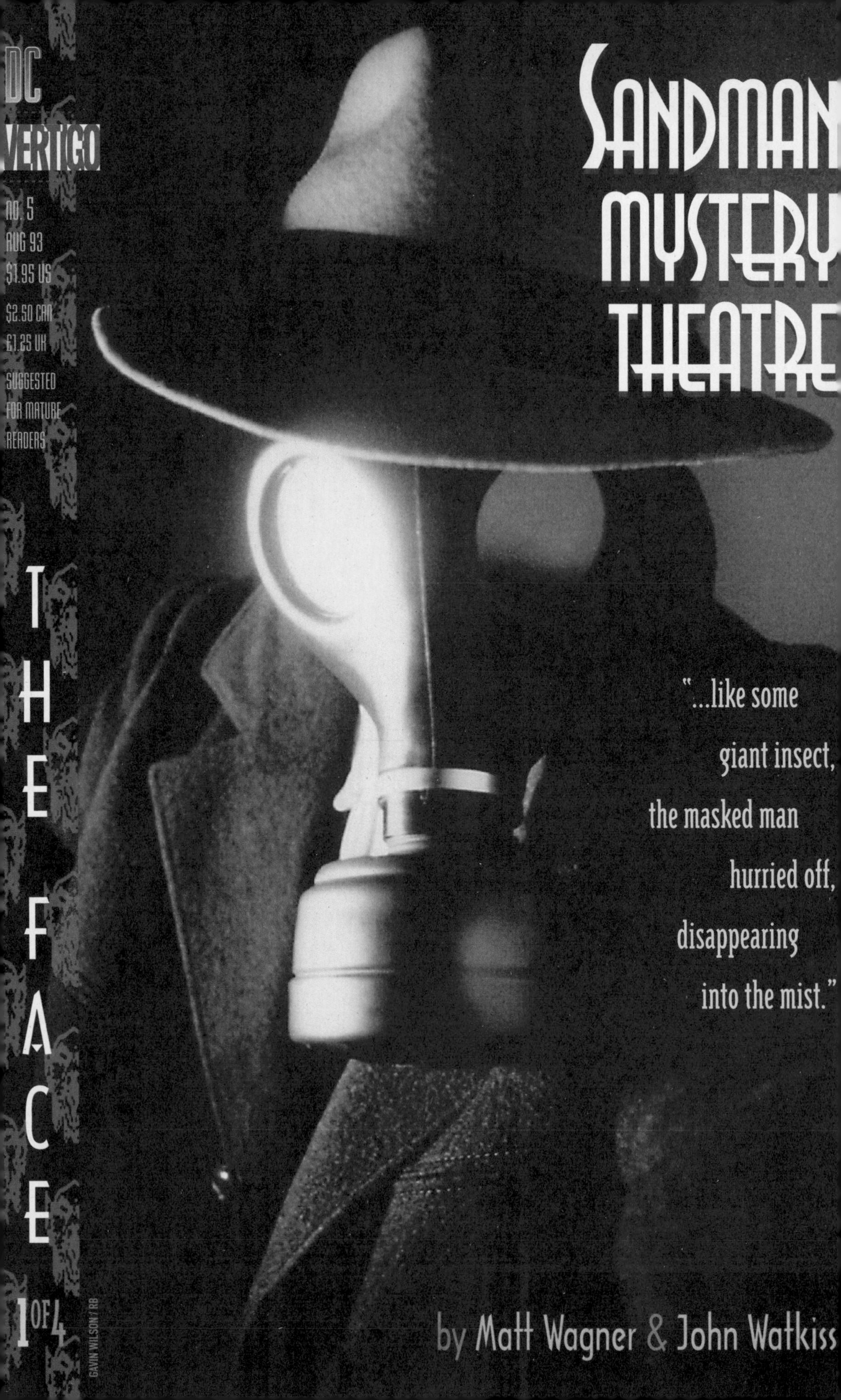
DC
VERTIGO
NO. 5
AUG 93
$1.95 US
$2.50 CAN
£1.25 UK
SUGGESTED FOR MATURE READERS
SANDMAN MYSTERY THEATRE
"...like some giant insect, the masked man hurried off, disappearing into the mist."
THE FACE
1 OF 4
GAVIN WILSON / RB
by Matt Wagner & John Watkiss

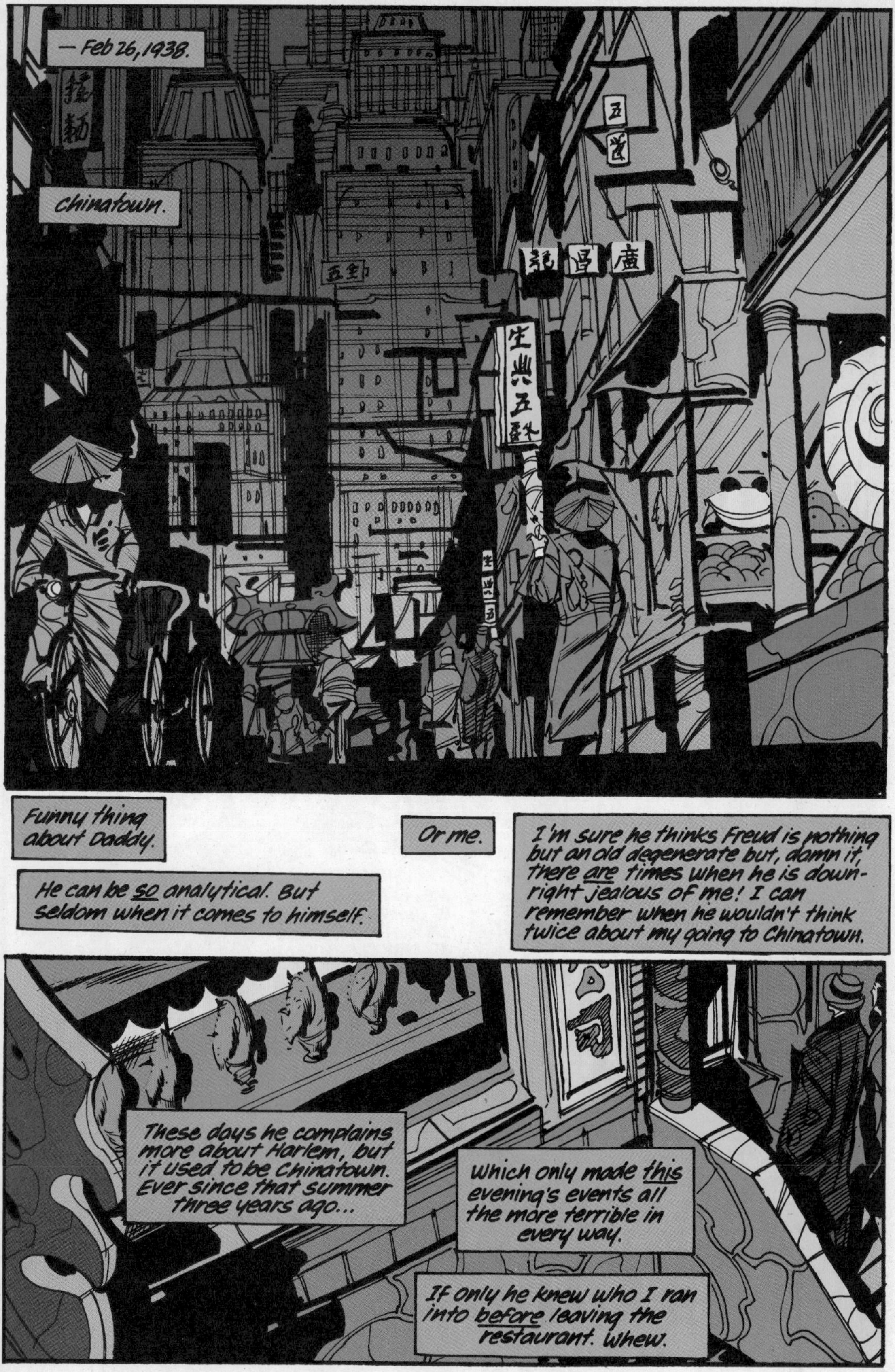
— Feb 26, 1938.
Chinatown.
Funny thing about Daddy.
He can be so analytical. But seldom when it comes to himself.
Or me.
I'm sure he thinks Freud is nothing but an old degenerate but, damn it, there are times when he is downright jealous of me! I can remember when he wouldn't think twice about my going to Chinatown.
These days he complains more about Harlem, but it used to be Chinatown. Ever since that summer three years ago...
Which only made this evening's events all the more terrible in every way.
If only he knew who I ran into before leaving the restaurant. Whew.

MMM... MMMM, I DO LOVE THIS STYLE OF COOKING!

YOU MEAN LETTING SOMEONE ELSE DO IT?

YOU ARE HUNGRY AGAIN IN AN HOUR, THOUGH. REALLY.

TOO SALTY.

AND TOO WEIRD-LOOKING FOR ME. WHEN'D YOU GET SUCH A TASTE FOR THIS STUFF, DIAN?

SEVERAL SUMMERS AGO.

DADDY INSISTED I TAKE A SUMMER JOB AS A LAW CLERK ON WALL STREET,

I USED TO COME OVER HERE WITH... ANOTHER CLERK FOR LUNCH SOMETIMES.

AND LUNCH LED TO DINNERS. AND DINNERS LED TO EVENINGS. AND EVENINGS AND EVENINGS AND EVENINGS.

HOW ARE YOU, DIAN?

J-JIMMY!!

WHAT ARE YOU... UHH-- I--I HAD HEARD YOU MOVED UP TO MIDTOWN?!

SO I DID.

BUT I'M HERE TO SEE A CLIENT WHO JUST SO HAPPENS TO OWN THIS PLACE,

ANNND... I DON'T WANT TO INTERRUPT YOUR EVENING OUT WITH FRIENDS.

OH! EXCUSE ME, EVERYONE...THIS IS JIMMY SHAN, AN OLD... FRIEND FROM MY LAW CLERK DAYS, IN FACT.

WILL YOU ALL EXCUSE US FOR JUST A MOMENT?

UMM-HMMMM...

The awful part is that I had avoided coming down here since then. And for the very same reason that lay beneath Daddy's griping.

②

JIMMY...

I'M SORRY. I...

IT'S OKAY, DIAN.

I DIDN'T MEAN TO TAKE YOU BY SURPRISE. I SAW YOU AS SOON AS I CAME IN AND JUST COULDN'T RESIST.

IT DOES SEEM LIKE SUCH A LONG TIME...

FAR TOO LONG. BUT I'M AFRAID I MEANT WHAT I SAID ABOUT BEING HERE ON BUSINESS TONIGHT.

CALL ME SOMETIME.

I MISS YOU, DIAN.

I--I WILL. GOODBYE, JIMMY.

WELLL... WE ARE ALL CERTAINLY WAITING...

SO, GIVE UP THE GOODS, GIRLIE.

ALL RIGHT, YES! WE... DATED FOR MOST OF THAT SUMMER I WAS HOME.

SOUNDS LIKE A HOT SUMMER.

WELL...

YOU'RE KIDDING.

WITH A CHINESE?!

YES, HE WAS DIFFERENT.

VERY PASSIONATE.

OKAY, SO SPILL. WHAT WAS IT LIKE?

WAS HE DIFFERENT? MORE...EXOTIC?

HE'S CANTONESE, SHELLY.

AND IF YOU MUST KNOW, TRISH...

IN FACT... I WOULD'VE THOUGHT HE WAS FRENCH.

:GASP:

WOO! WOO!!

OH, DIAN!!

(giggle)

3

It was only while teasing the gang that I realized the truth-- I *had* missed Jimmy, more than I cared to admit.

There have been a few other men in my life since then, but none quite like Jimmy.

Daddy hated him.

< GREETINGS, WU SUNG. >

< AND TO YOU, ZHANG CHAI LAO. PEACE TO THE LEI FENG AND ALL THEIR FAMILIES. >

< AND TO THE HUO YIBAI. THAT IS OUR INTENT, ANYHOW, IN ANSWERING YOUR SUMMONS. >

< AS IS OUR INTENT IN VOICING IT. >

< THERE IS A COMEDIAN, LING HOON, COUSIN TO A HIGH MAN IN THE LEI FENG. HE PERFORMS AT THE DOYER ST. THEATER? >

< HE IS HSU CHANG'S SECOND COUSIN. >

< YES. >

< AND HE'S GOT A BIG MOUTH. >

< THIS COMEDIAN HAS LEVELED HIS HUMOR AT US OF LATE, IF ONE CALLS SUCH GARBAGE HUMOR. >

< HE DISGRACES OUR WOMEN WITH FILTHY TALK. AND IMPLIES THAT OUR SERVICES ARE LESS THAN ADEQUATE. HIS INNUENDO IS BECOMING KNOWN IN EVERY HOUSEHOLD. >

< MY ELDERS HAVE INSTRUCTED ME TO SAY THIS COMEDIAN WILL BE REPRIMANDED. WE HAVE NO WISH TO BRING SHAME TO THE HUO YIBAI. >

< THINGS THAT ARE PAST, IT IS NEEDLESS TO BLAME. >

4

AHH... THANKS FOR COMING TONIGHT, EVERYONE. I REALLY NEEDED IT.

NO PROBLEM, DIAN.

YES, I LOVE CHINATOWN TOO, I MUST ADMIT. IT'S ALL JUST SO DIFFERENT AND QUAINT.

I DON'T LIKE BEING WHERE I CAN'T READ ANYTHING. GIVES ME THE WILLIES.

SPEAKING OF WHICH, DO YOU KNOW WHERE WE'RE STANDING?

THIS CORNER'S CALLED THE BLOODY ANGLE.

USED TO BE SAID MORE MURDERS WERE COMMITTED HERE THAN ANY OTHER SITE ON AMERICA-A-AAHH!

OH. DON'T BE SILLY. IT'S JUST ONE OF THOSE EXOTIC MASKS THEY MAKE. MUST BE THEIR NEW YEAR'S OR SOMETHING.

THEIRS IS DIFFERENT FROM OURS, YOU KNOW.

AND ABOUT TWICE AS OLD, CAROL. I WOULDN'T DISTURB THA--

OH, I WON'T HURT ANYTHIN- (gasp)!

Daddy told me to stay out of chinatown.

⑤

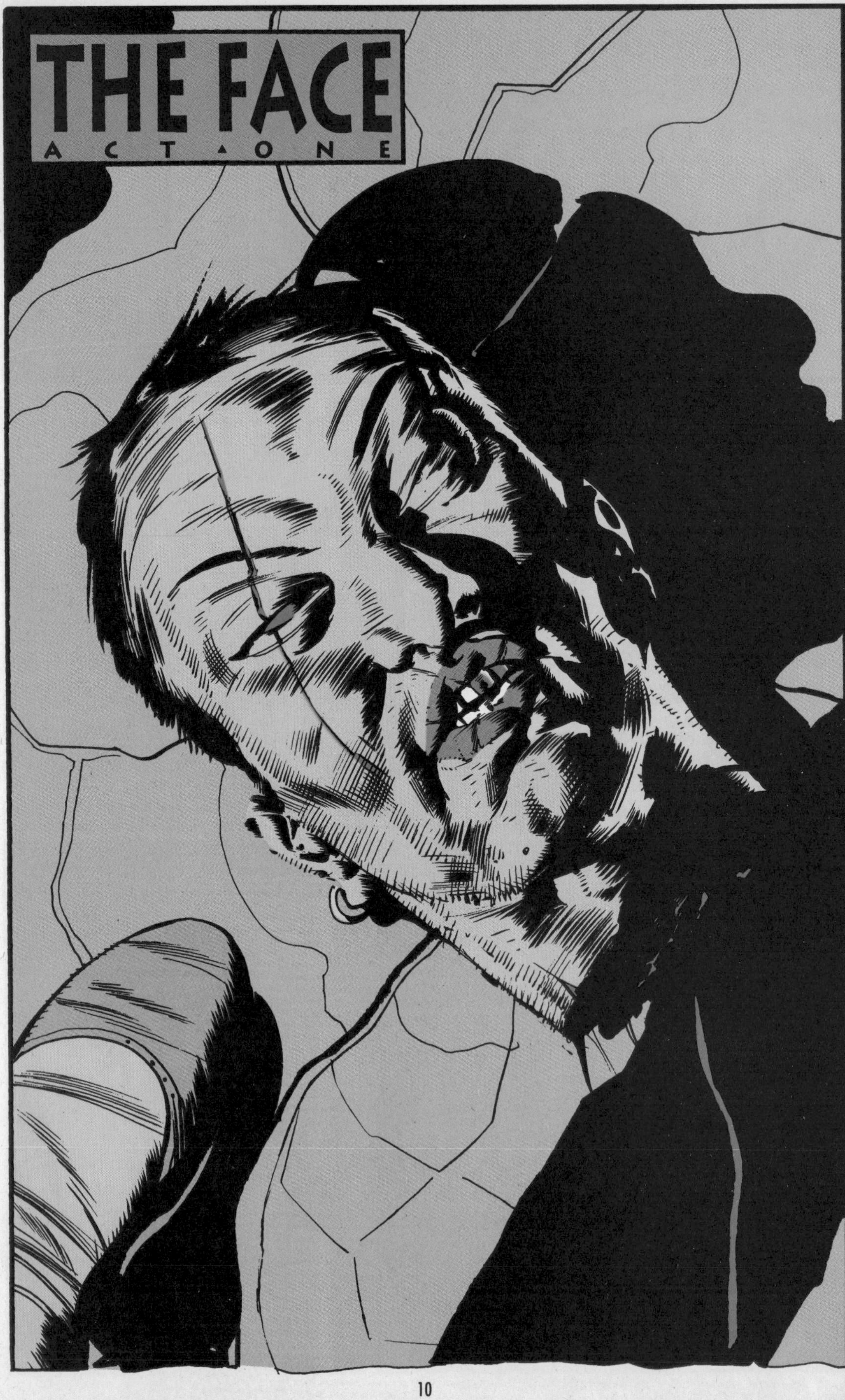
THE FACE
ACT • ONE

COME, MY DEAR...

I'M HERE TO TAKE YOU OUT OF THIS HORRID PLACE.

FINALLY...

Of course, Daddy insisted on coming to pick me up at the scene himself. My friends had all been taken home, but I had to wait with the police.

SO...YOU RECOGNIZE THIS, UHH...FACE?

HIM DRIVE TRUCK FOR LIL' SAM SUNG.

JUST A TRUCK DRIVER. *UH?* YEAH, MY ASS.

DADDY...?

WHY ARE THERE SO MANY POLICE HERE, TONIGHT? I COUNTED ALMOST *TWENTY* SQUAD CARS FOR A SINGLE HOMICIDE?

DIAN, PLEASE, GET IN THE CAR.

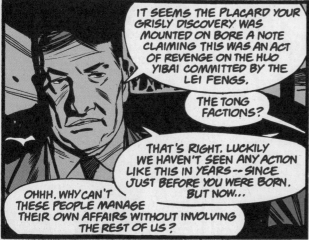

IT SEEMS THE PLACARD YOUR GRISLY DISCOVERY WAS MOUNTED ON BORE A NOTE CLAIMING THIS WAS AN ACT OF REVENGE ON THE HUO YIBAI COMMITTED BY THE LEI FENGS.

THE TONG FACTIONS?

THAT'S RIGHT. LUCKILY WE HAVEN'T SEEN ANY ACTION LIKE THIS IN YEARS -- SINCE JUST BEFORE YOU WERE BORN. BUT NOW...

OHHH. WHY CAN'T THESE PEOPLE MANAGE THEIR OWN AFFAIRS WITHOUT INVOLVING THE REST OF US?

THE LAW IS STILL A WHITE WORLD, DADDY.

NOW, DIAN...

7

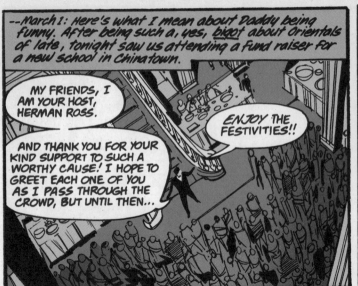

--March 1: Here's what I mean about Daddy being funny. After being such a, yes, _bigot_ about Orientals of late, tonight saw us attending a fund raiser for a new school in Chinatown.

MY FRIENDS, I AM YOUR HOST, HERMAN ROSS.

ENJOY THE FESTIVITIES!!

AND THANK YOU FOR YOUR KIND SUPPORT TO SUCH A WORTHY CAUSE! I HOPE TO GREET EACH ONE OF YOU AS I PASS THROUGH THE CROWD, BUT UNTIL THEN...

HERMAN, NICE TO SEE YOU.

I THINK YOU'VE MET MY DAUGHTER, DIAN?

YES, OF COURSE, OF COURSE. SO GOOD OF YOU BOTH TO COME AND SHOW YOUR SUPPORT FOR THE ORIENTAL COMMUNITY.

IT'S OUR PLEASURE, MR. ROSS.

MAY BE _YOUR_ PLEASURE, M' DEAR; BUT YOUR FATHER THINKS I NEVER NOTICED THAT HIS NAME WASN'T ON OUR GUEST LIST TILL SEVERAL DAYS AGO.

DOESN'T MATTER, WE'LL TAKE SUPPORT ANYWHERE WE CAN FIND IT! _HAW, HAW!_

Daddy had claimed his attendance was at the mayor's request--public relations, especially now.

HERMAN! I NEED YOU TO POINT THAT GLAD HAND IN THIS DIRECTION FOR A WHILE.

MEET WESLEY DODDS.

WELL, I, UM...

MR. DODDS IS _VERY_ INTERESTED IN PATRONIZING OUR SCHOOL.

MR. ROSS.

THAT'S WONDERFUL, BENSON!

SO, MY WILY PARTNER'S ROPED YOU INTO THE GOOD FIGHT--_EH_, DODDS? WE APPRECIATE THE SUPPORT!

ALWAYS READY TO HELP, SIR. I BELIEVE YOU KNEW MY FATHER?

EDWARD DODDS?

WELL, I CERTAINLY DID! SERVED IN THE GREAT WAR WITH HIM! I WAS SORRY TO HEAR HE'D PASSED AWAY.

A CHARITABLE MAN.

I'LL BE RIGHT BACK, DIAN.

8

HE'D BE PROUD TO SEE THAT THE TRADITION'S LIVED ON. EH?

THANK YOU, SIR.

GOT YOUR HOOKS IN ANOTHER ONE, HERMAN?

CAREFUL, MY FRIEND...

A PROLONGED EXPOSURE TO HERMAN ROSS WILL LEAVE YOUR BANK ACCOUNT FEELING EMPTY.

JIMMY, M'BOY!

HOW ARE YOU? HOW ARE YOU?

VERY WELL, THANKS. AND HOW GOES THE DRIVE FOR OUR SCHOOL?

SMOOTHER THANKS TO YOUR HELP. JIMMY SHAN, HERE, HELPED ARRANGE THE PURCHASE OF OUR SCHOOL BUILDING! OH, THIS IS WESLEY DO...

I KNOW MISS BELMONT ALREADY.

HELLO AGAIN, JIMMY.

I HEARD ABOUT THE OTHER NIGHT, CALL ME.

LOOKS GOOD, HERMAN.

BE SPEAKING TO YOU SOON. EVENING, MR...?

DODDS.

CERTAINLY, M'BOY.

WELL, I'M OFF TO WORK THIS CROWD MYSELF.

GOOD EVENING, EVERY- ONE.

SO THEN, MR. WESLEY DODDS... LONG TIME NO SEE.

⑨

HOW 'VE YOU BEE-- UH... WESLEY?

WES!

WES, WHAT IS IT? WHAT'S WRONG? YOU WERE... STARING AFTER JIMMY. HE'S JUST AN OLD FRIEND.

I... DIDN'T THINK THAT WOULD BOTHER YOU...

YOU MEAN BECAUSE HE'S CANTONESE?!

DIAN, I ALL BUT GREW UP IN THE ORIENT. IN CERTAIN WAYS YOU APPEAR STRANGER TO ME THAN ANY ASIAN WOULD.

OH.

WELL... IT'S JUST THAT YOU WERE RATHER QUIET EARLIER AND THEN...

WELL, JIMMY DOES COME ON STRONG AT TIMES.

I MERELY THOUGHT I RECOGNIZED HIM AND I WAS TRYING TO RECALL FROM WHERE.

10

CATHERINE? STILL SPENDING TIME IN THE COUNTRY MAINLY. I SAW HER AROUND A WEEK AGO AND SHE LOOKED MUCH BETTER.

BUT IT IS NICE TO SEE YOU AGAIN -- AND UNDER BETTER CIRCUMSTANCES. HOW IS YOUR FRIEND DOING?

GOOD TO HEAR. THE SOONER SHE CAN FORGET THAT DREADFUL BUSINESS THE BETTER.

AND SO, WOULD YOU CARE TO JOIN ME FOR A DRINK?

YOU? DRINK?

I FIGURE THE PUNCH BOWL AT A SCHOOL CHARITY BALL HAS A DECENT CHANCE OF REMAINING UN-SPIKED.

UH-UH. GUESS AGAIN, YOU DESERT.

GROOOAN-- MAYBE JUST A SELTZER, THEN.

Still shaken from seeing Jimmy twice in such a short time period, I spent most of the evening with Wesley Dodds.

He's a very serious sort, but also relaxed and confident in his own way. Says he's a dreamer. I believe it.

Funny thing. Daddy somehow managed to avoiding running into Jimmy even once all evening long. Imagine that.

⑪

< I HEARD THE OTHER DAY ABOUT A BAKER WHO WAS HUO YIBAI. >

< HE COULDN'T MAKE HIS DOUGH TO RISE IN THE MORNING... >

< ...AND SO HIS LOAF HAD GONE FLAT BY THE NIGHT! >

< OR SO HIS WIFE IS SAID TO CLAIM... >

CLAPCLAPCLAPCLAP

< VERY GOOD SHOW, LING HOON. >

< YOU SHOULD HAVE EXPECTED NOTHING LESS. >

KNOCK KNOCK

< WHO IS IT? >

< LAUNDRY, SIR. >

< YOU ARE LATE! I WANTED THAT DELIVERED BEFORE MY PERFORMANCE TONIGHT. >

< I KNOW, SIR. SO SORRY, SIR. >

< SEE THAT YOU ARE MORE CAREFUL NEXT TIME. >

12

< I AM A GREAT COMEDIAN, YOU KNOW. AND MY APPEARANCE IS PART OF MY SUCCESS. >

< YES, SIR, I REALIZE THAT, SIR. >

< YOU SEE... >

< I KNOW ALL ABOUT APPEARANCES AND SUCH. >

KNOCK-KNOCK-

YES, COME IN?

All in all, the evening had left me with a strange feeling of resolve.

JUST ME.

I WANTED TO SAY GOOD NIGHT AND THANKS FOR JOINING ME THIS EVENING. I DO HATE HAVING TO DO PUBLICITY STINTS FOR CITY HALL SOMETIMES.

YOU'RE WELCOME, DADDY. GOOD NIGHT.

More than ever, I was determined to go see Jimmy on my own again.

Suddenly, it felt like part of me was missing.

⑬

<"GENTLEMEN, PLACE YOUR BETS.">

<"FIFTY AND RAISE YOU THIRTY.">

<"SEVENTY-FIVE ON THE RED.">

<"FOR YOU, HANDSOME, ONLY TEN.">

<"BLACK SEVENTEEN.">

<"TWENTY-ONE!">

<"EIGHT, NINE, TWENTY THOUSAND.">

<FIVE, SIX, SEVEN, EIGHT, NINE...>

<...TWENTY-ONE THOUSAND. FIVE, SIX, SEVEN, EIGHT, NINE...>

<...TWENTY-TWO THOUSAND.>

<FIVE, SIX, SEVEN, EIGHT...>

KLUNK

<UHN.>

<NINE-- THE ROOF. TWENTY-THREE THOUSAND. FIVE, SIX, SEVEN...>

14

< THIRTY THOUSAND. >

< THAT WAS FAST. FIND ANYTHING? FIVE, SIX, SEV-- >

< YES. >

< I HAVE FOUND ONE WHO MIGHT HAVE THE ANSWERS I SEEK. YOU ARE MASTER BEI? >

< I SEEK INFORMATION ON THE MIGHTY TONGS... >

< ...AND WHERE BETTER THAN FROM SUCH A RESPECTED MASTER OF SECRETS? >

< MY HOUSE IS WELL-KNOWN IN SOME CIRCLES AND MY FACE, AS YOU CAN SEE, IS UNMASKED. >

< ASK. I MAY ANSWER. >

< WHY IS THERE SUCH VIOLENCE IN THE AIR? >

< NO ONE SEEMS TO KNOW. >

< THE BOY WHOSE HEAD THEY FOUND WAS MUO YIBAI BUT THE LEI FENG DENY KILLING HIM. >

< THERE WAS A NOTE. >

< A FORGERY. >

< THE LEI FENG LEADERS HAVE MANAGED TO CONVINCE WU SUNG OF THAT, BUT ONLY JUST. THE SITUATION IS HOT. >

‹WHO STANDS TO BENEFIT THE MOST FROM SUCH A WAR?›

‹NO ONE, REALLY. THE OTHER SOCIETIES ARE NOT STRONG ENOUGH.›

‹THEN WHO IS BEHIND IT ALL? WHO DID THE KILLING?›

‹THIS IS NOT KNOWN.›

‹IN FACT, MAYBE IT WAS SOMEONE OUTSIDE OF CHINATOWN.›

‹A STRANGER AMONGST US--DISGUISED, PERHAPS, MAYBE, SOMEONE LIKE...›

‹...YOU!!›

‹THIS ONE THANKS MASTER BE! FOR HIS HONESTY, IF NOT FOR HIS SUSPICIONS.›

‹KOFF-HACK!! LING HO, COME AT ONCE!!›

‹NOTHING ON THE ROOF, BOSS-- WHAT?! IS IT A FIRE?!!›

‹HACK! HACK!!›

‹NO--KOFF, KOFF!! G-GET... GET HIM...HACK! HACK! HACK!›

‹WHO?--:COFF, COFF, HACK! HACK!›

16

BZZZZ

HELLO, JIMMY.

DIAN!

I DIDN'T EXPECT TO HEAR FROM YOU SO... EASILY.

PLEASE, COME IN.

I'M A BIT SURPRISED MYSELF.

THIS IS A NICE PLACE YOU HAVE.

IT'S OKAY. I KNOW THE BUILDING'S NOT EXACTLY THE RITZ.

BUT I'VE FIXED THIS APARTMENT UP AND IT'S CERTAINLY BETTER THAN ANYTHING MY PARENTS EVER HAD. PLEASE, HAVE A SEAT.

CARE FOR A DRINK?

IN A BIT. SO... HOW ARE THINGS?

VERY WELL. I'VE BEEN WORKING WITH MY UNCLE'S FAMILY FOR QUITE SOME TIME NOW.

MY LAW TRAINING COMES IN HANDY BUT SO FAR IT HASN'T BEEN NECESSARY TO SIT FOR THE BAR.

YOUR UNCLE'S FAMILY... ARE THEY A "TONG"?

OH, DIAN... SUCH ANTIQUATED TERMS YOU USE. TONGS ARE REALLY A THING OF THE PAST. THIS IS MORE OF A MUTUAL AID SOCIETY.

RING! RING!

RATHER LIKE A UNION. OH... EXCUSE ME.

17

HELLO?

BZZZZ

PACKAGE FOR MR. SHAN?

HE'S ON THE PHONE. I'LL TAKE IT, THANKS.

HERMAN! YES, GOOD TO HEAR FROM YOU,

YES, WE COULD MEET THIS AFTERNOON TO DISCUSS THOSE DETAILS... CERTAINLY... I WILL...

SEE YOU THEN, HERMAN...

WHAT'S THIS?

A PARCEL FOR YOU.

SHOPPING SEARS & ROEBUCK THESE DAYS, JIMMY?

NO... WHAT COULD THIS BE?

YOU'RE QUITE IN-VOLVED WITH THAT NEW SCHOOL, AREN'T YOU?

IF MY PEOPLE ARE TO LIVE IN THIS COUNTRY, THEY MUST LEARN ALL THEY CAN FROM IT.

THIS IS THE FIRST STEP TO GETTING A--

...AHEA--

JIMMY, WHAT'S WRONG? WHAT'S IN THE BO--

UMM... FINE.

I MUST GET READY TO MEET MESSRS. ROSS AND BENSON FOR LUNCH, NOW, DIAN.

HOW ABOUT DINNER FRIDAY NIGHT?

GOOD! CALL ME TOMORROW?

Y-YES, OF COURSE.

GOOD. GOOD! SEE YOU THEN!

18

...F'I DI'NT KNOOOOW, WHA I DI'NT KNOOOOW-- HIC-- DEN I WOO 'NT KNOOOOW, WHA I WOO'NT KNOWWWW...

≈HIC≈

CUTE, YOU ARE LATE AGAIN...

AND YOU SMELL.

NO, YOU SMELL. I STINK--GOD-DAMN ILLITERATE FLUNKY.

BUT HE'S RIGHT. YOU ARE LATE.

SO WHAT?

SO YOU HAVE TO SIT ON YOUR FAT ASS IN HERE AN EXTRA HALF-HOUR WHILE BRUISER-BOY HAS TO WAIT OUT IN THE COLD DARK ALLEY? OOO, MY MASCARA'S RUNNIN'.

YOU GOT WHAT YOU PAID FOR.

TRUE ENOUGH.

AND NOW WE MUST WAIT FOR RESULTS, LIE LOW UNTIL THEN. HAVE SOME FUN. BUT STAY IN TOWN A WHILE LONGER.

THERE SHALL BE MORE WORK FOR YOU.

THERE'S ALWAYS WORK WITH MEN LIKE YOU AROUND, FAT ASS.

SEE YOU THEN.

I WILL CONTACT YOU BY THE NORMAL MEANS.

UH-HUH.

LET'S GO, DRIVER.

⑲

< I'VE GOT WHAT ANY SLUT LIKE YOU IS AFTER. >

< BUT HAVE YOU GOT WHAT I NEED TONIGHT? >

I GOT IT ALL, I DO IT ALL, BABY. FIVE BUCKS.

WELL, WELL, WELL...

WHAT HAVE WE HERE?

< SOLD. >

< LIAN. >

THEN, FOLLOW ME... WHAT'S YOUR NAME?

FACE? GOOFY NAME. BUT YOU LOOK FINE TO ME, HANDSOME.

UH-HUH.

WHAT'S UP?

FOLDIN' YOUR CLOTHES? SAY, AIN'T YOU A NEAT ONE? COME ON, LET'S GO ALREADY.

< I LIKE THINGS TO BE IN THEIR PROPER PLACE. >

< YOU'LL SEE. >

OHH, NO, NO, NO...

SHUT UP.

NO, WAIT-A-MINUTE, JUNIOR! I'LL SCREAM! I MEAN IT--

20

< HOW MUCH DID WE SAY, AGAIN? >

; sob-sob-sob-sob ;

; sob-sob-sob-sob ;

B-B-BASTARD...

BASTARD! Y-YOU T-TORE ME UP! I-I'LL B-BE WORTHLESS--

AGGHHH--

< WORTH? I'D SAY TEN CENTS AT BEST. >

GET OUT! YOU MONSTER!! YOU BASTARD, GET OUT!!

< NOW, NOW... NOTHING TO LOSE YOUR PRETTY HEAD ABOUT. >

WHAT IS IT?!

WHAT'S IT SAY?!

IT'S A DECLARATION OF WAR-- BY THE LEI FENG!

21

KNOCK
KNOCK

YES?

I had spent the rest of the afternoon idling in and out of shops. Trying to forget about Jimmy's odd behavior.

HI, DADDY! JUST THOUGHT I'D SEE IF YOU WANTED TO HAVE DINN—

OH!... I'M SORRY.

MA'AM.

MISS BELMONT.

LIEUTENANT, GENTLEMEN.

NO, I'M AFRAID I'LL BE RATHER LATE AGAIN, DEAR. THERE'S BEEN SOME FURTHER TONG ACTIVITY.

BUT I HAD HEARD THAT THE TONGS WERE REALLY NO LONGER ACTIVE. THAT THEY--

WHERE ON EARTH DID YOU EVER HEAR THAT?!

WELL, AT... THE OTHER NIGHT, AT THE CHARITY BALL.

PROBABLY SOME OF HERMAN ROSS'S HOOEY.

WELL, TWO HORRIBLE MURDERS AND A PUBLICLY POSTED CHALLENGE HAVE LEFT US ALL DOWNTOWN FINDING THE TONGS ALL TOO REAL.

NOW, BE A DARLING AND PROMISE ME YOU'LL TAKE A CAB HOME FROM HERE, YES?

Not bad enough being turned down and ushered out by two men in one day... but who'd believe three?!

WELL, NOW, FANCY MEETING YOU HERE, STRANGER!

HMM... OH, HELLO, DIAN?

VISITING YOUR FATHER?

THAT'S RIGHT. HE'S WORKING LATE.

ACTUALLY, I WAS LOOKING FOR A DINNER COMPANION.

WHAT DO YOU SAY? CARE TO JOIN ME?

BOY, I'D LOVE TO BUT I CAN'T. I HAVE TO WORK LATE TONIGHT MYSELF. IN FACT, I WAS JUST CHECKING SOME PROPERTY RECORDS AT THE COURTHOUSE.

(groooan) ARE ALL MEN SUCH TERRIBLE WORK-HORSES?

SOME OF US. THE OTHERS HAVE NO IMAGINATION.

BUT, LISTEN, WE DO SEEM TO HAVE A HABIT OF STRAYING INTO EACH OTHER. SO I'LL TAKE A RAIN CHECK ON THAT DINNER. OKAY?

(sigh) OKAY. WELL, UNTIL THEN...

GOOD NIGHT, DIAN.

Wesley's enterprise was the same quality that had eventually come between Jimmy and me (even more than Daddy). They are both just so damn driven in life. Why have I never had such definite goals?

Of the two, though, Wesley is the more mysterious. I don't really think Jimmy has much imagination, only desire (and plenty of that).

Wesley continually says he has dreams.

23

27

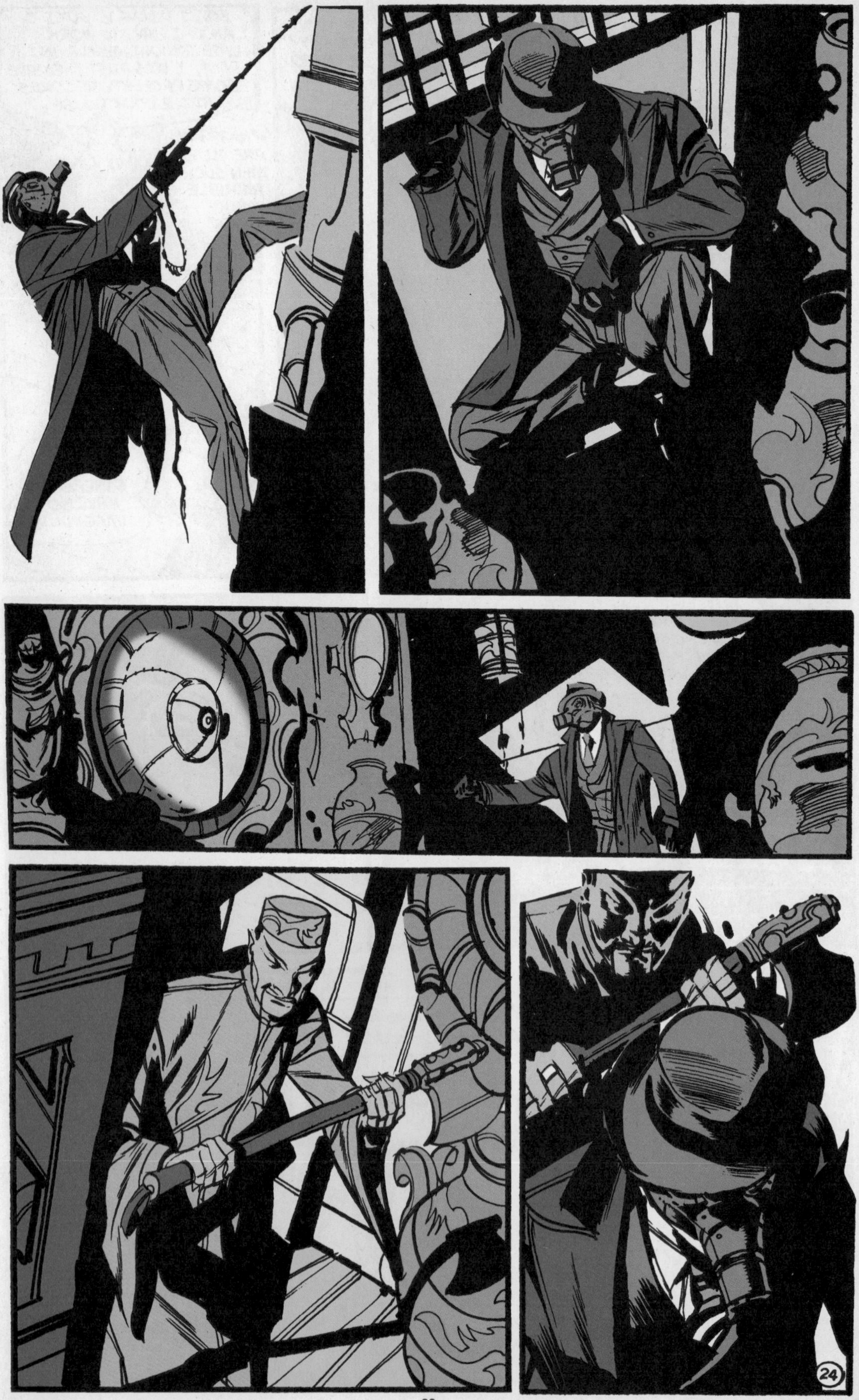
24

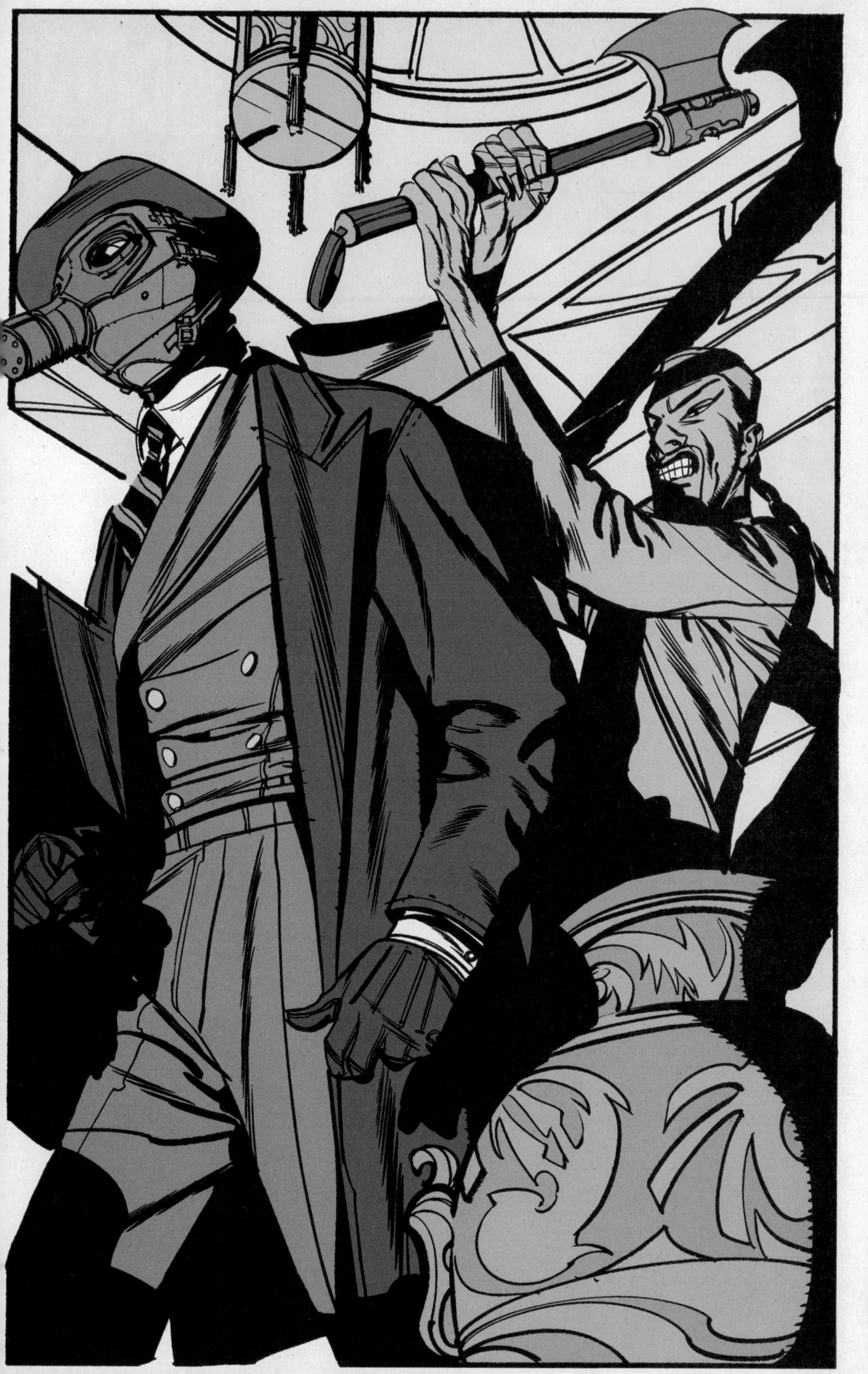

DC
VERTIGO
NO. 6
SEP 93
$1.95 US
$2.50 CAN
£1.25 UK
SUGGESTED FOR MATURE READERS
SANDMAN MYSTERY THEATRE
by Matt Wagner & John Watkiss
THE FACE
2 OF 4
"...the blade bit deeply into the soft flesh of the throat, snapping the gristly tendons."
GAVIN WILSON / RB

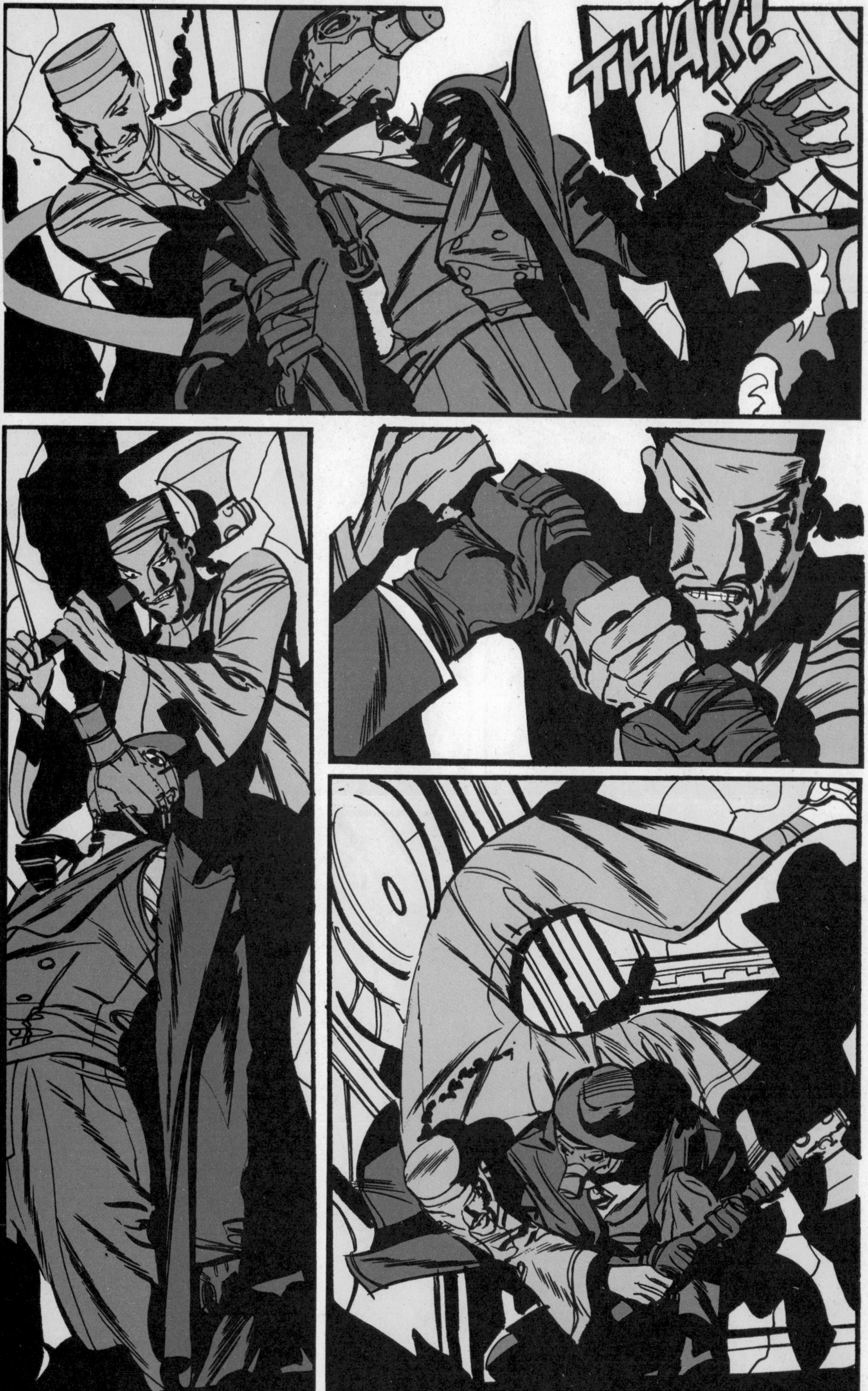
THAK!

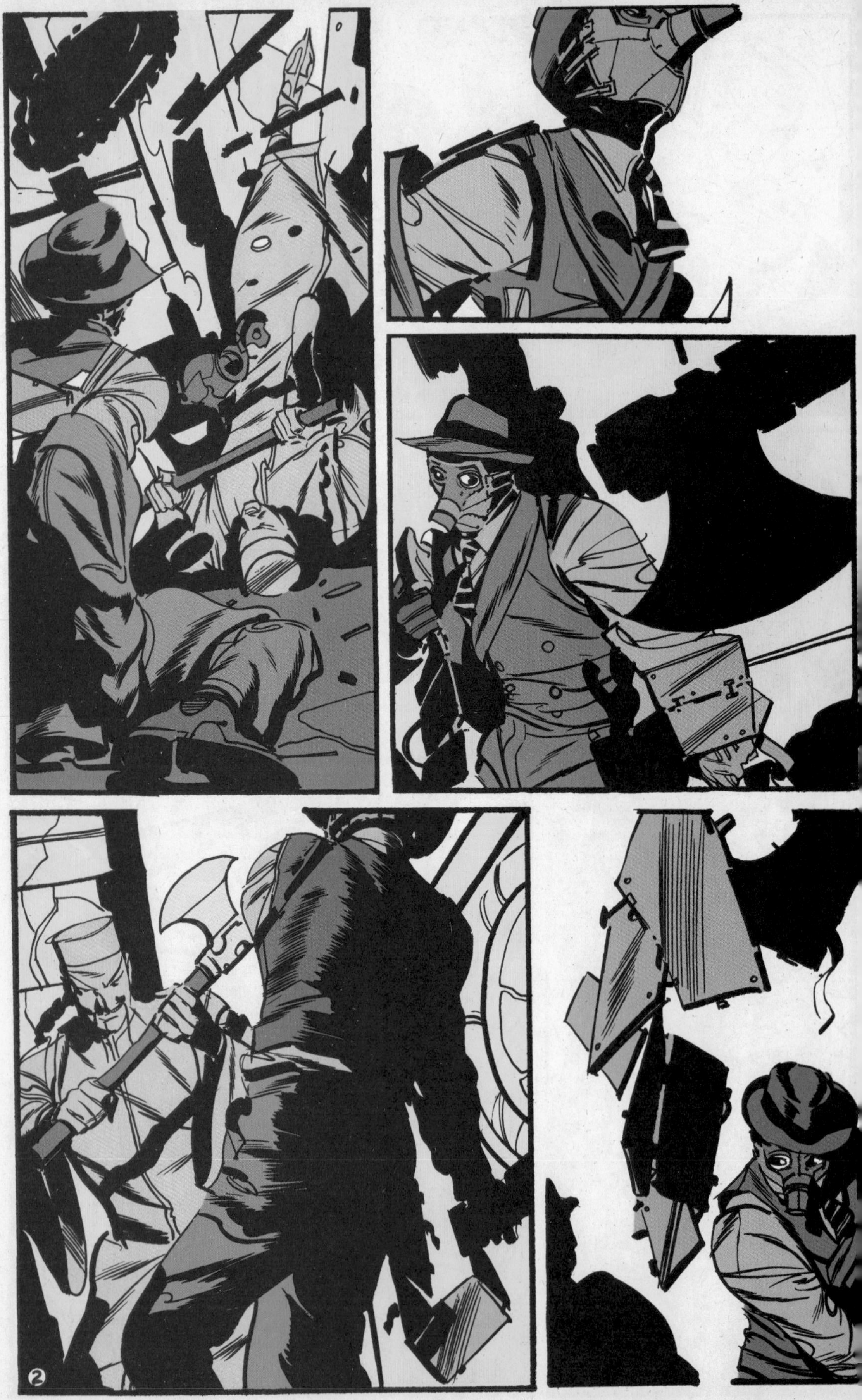
2

KLAK-ANGGG!

FOOSH...

<KOFF!>

<HACK! KOFF!>

<THE HUO YIBAI ARE INNOCENT. OUR WAR STANCE AGAINST THEM IS UNFOUNDED.>

③

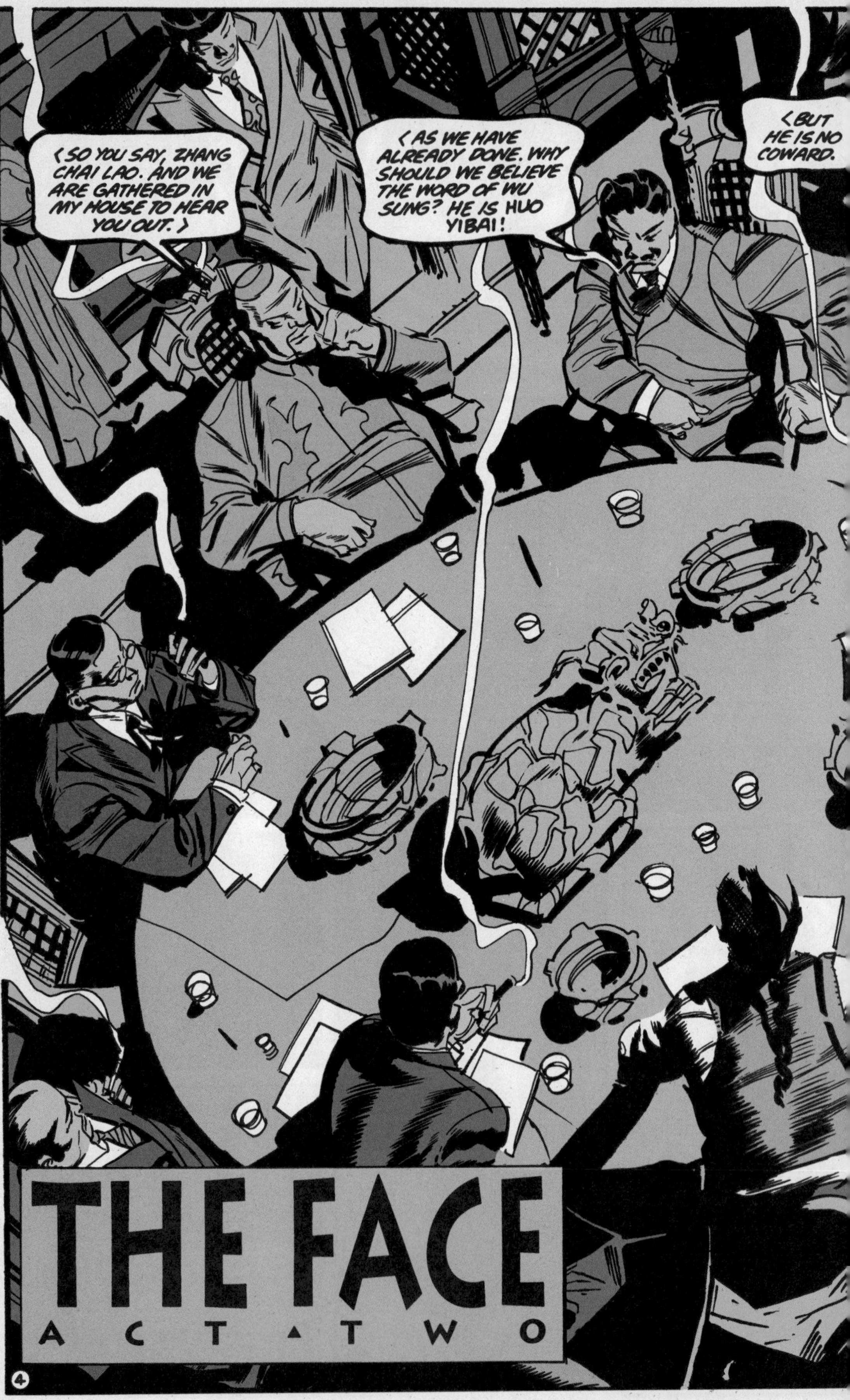

<SO YOU SAY, ZHANG CHAI LAO. AND WE ARE GATHERED IN MY HOUSE TO HEAR YOU OUT.>
<AS WE HAVE ALREADY DONE. WHY SHOULD WE BELIEVE THE WORD OF WU SUNG? HE IS HUO YIBAI!
<BUT HE IS NO COWARD.
THE FACE
ACT TWO
4

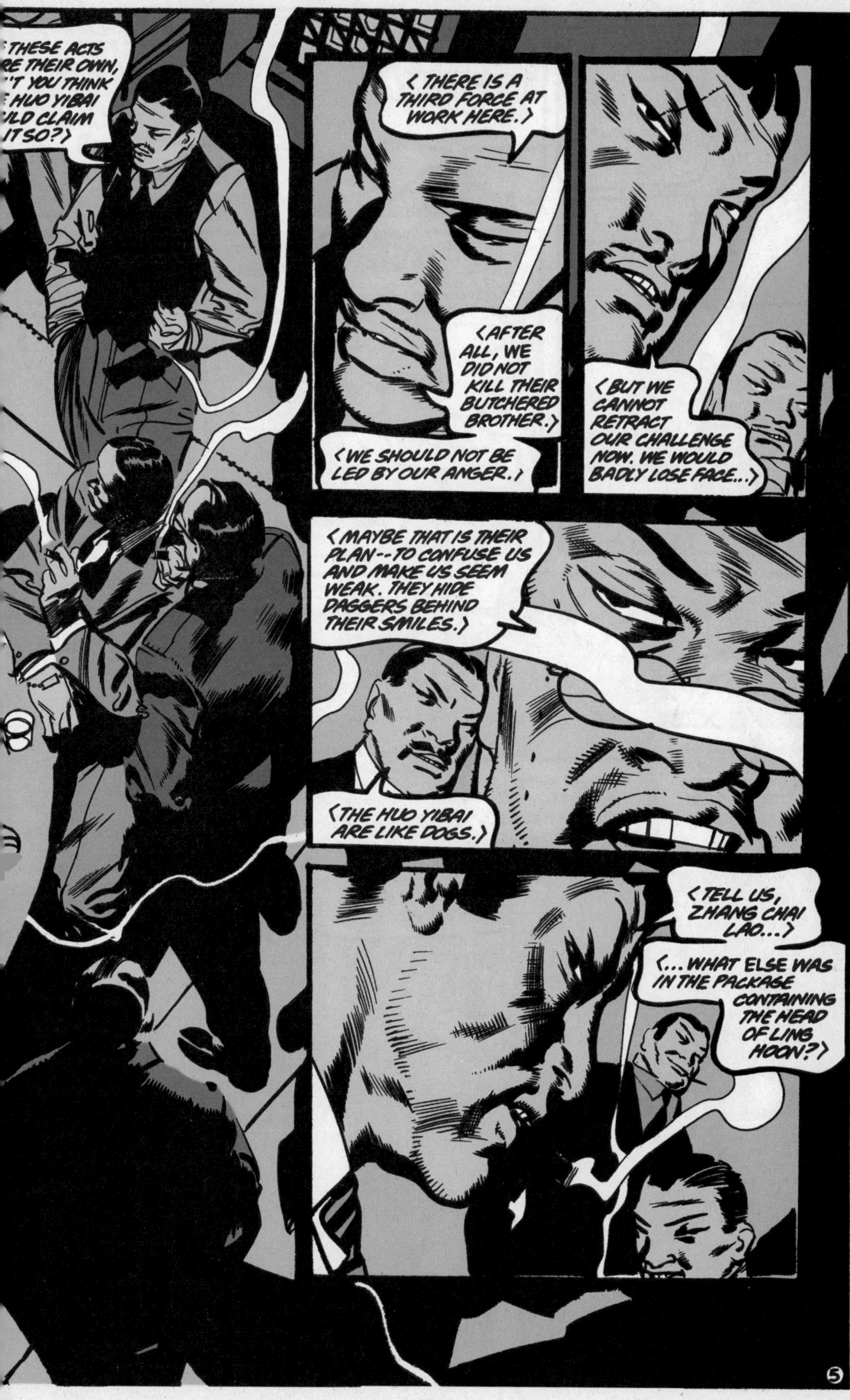
F THESE ACTS RE THEIR OWN, 'T YOU THINK E HUO YIBAI ULD CLAIM IT SO?>
<THERE IS A THIRD FORCE AT WORK HERE.>
<AFTER ALL, WE DID NOT KILL THEIR BUTCHERED BROTHER.>
<WE SHOULD NOT BE LED BY OUR ANGER.>
<BUT WE CANNOT RETRACT OUR CHALLENGE NOW. WE WOULD BADLY LOSE FACE...>
<MAYBE THAT IS THEIR PLAN--TO CONFUSE US AND MAKE US SEEM WEAK. THEY HIDE DAGGERS BEHIND THEIR SMILES.>
<THE HUO YIBAI ARE LIKE DOGS.>
<TELL US, ZHANG CHAI LAO...>
<...WHAT ELSE WAS IN THE PACKAGE CONTAINING THE HEAD OF LING HOON?>
5

‹THE--UH... HE--›

‹HIS... HIS TESTICLES WERE STUFFED INTO THE MOUTH.›

‹BUT--›

‹AND THEY HAD ALREADY COMPLAINED ABOUT HIS JOKES!›

‹HSU CHANG, THIS MAN WAS YOUR COUSIN!›

‹IS THERE ANY DOUBT HE WAS MURDERED BY OUR ENEMIES?›

‹LING HOON'S HUMOR WAS VULGAR. PERHAPS HIS ENEMIES ARE NOT OUR OWN-- EH?›

‹WHAT?!›

‹DEATH TO THE HUO YIBAI!!›

‹HONORED GUESTS, HERE IS EVIL NEWS. AN INTRUDER HAS BEEN DRIVEN OFF WHILE SPYING ON THIS MEETING!!›

‹THEY HAVE INVADED MY VERY HOUSE!!›

‹THEY WILL LIE IN RUINOUS DEFEAT!!›

Jimmy always said his people's history was a mixture of rage in the name of order...

And death in the name of pride.

TOO MANY HANGOVERS AND NOT ENOUGH MEN.

I finally found an evening partner in Carol Swanson. I now realize that this was an effort not to think about Jimmy. Capricious and vain, she is unlike him in almost every way.

SO, CAROL, WHAT'S NEW AND EXCITING IN YOUR LIFE?

OR, I SHOULD SAY, NOT ENOUGH GOOD ONES. YOU STILL SEEING THE CHINAMAN?

WELL...NOT REALLY. BUT WE DO HAVE A DATE THIS FRIDAY NIGHT.

LIKE ROBERT MONTGOMERY...

I DON'T KNOW HOW YOU DO IT, SISTER. I LIKE MINE WHITE. WHITE AND HANDSOME. POWERFUL'S GOOD, TOO.

TO EACH HER OWN, CAROL.

LADIES AND GENTLEMEN, THE PALAIS ROYALE IS PROUD TO BRING YOU THE SWINGING SOUNDS OF--

--THE ARTIE SHAW BAND! C'MON ALL YOU "JITTER-BUGGERS!"

GOOD GOD...

LOOK AT THEM GO.

AS IF I NEED ANOTHER REASON TO FEEL ANY OLDER.

WHERE DO THEY GET THE ENERGY? I MEAN I'VE SEEN THIS TYPE OF THING IN HARLEM...

...BUT *THERE* IT ALWAYS FEELS SO FUN--SO FREE.

HERE, ALL THE ACROBATICS JUST SEEM SO...

...DESPERATE.

As I gazed at the dancers, I couldn't help feeling ashamed. Wasn't I guilty of the same frivolity, after all?

Don't I really *know* what I glimpsed inside that box at Jimmy's.

Ⓑ

38

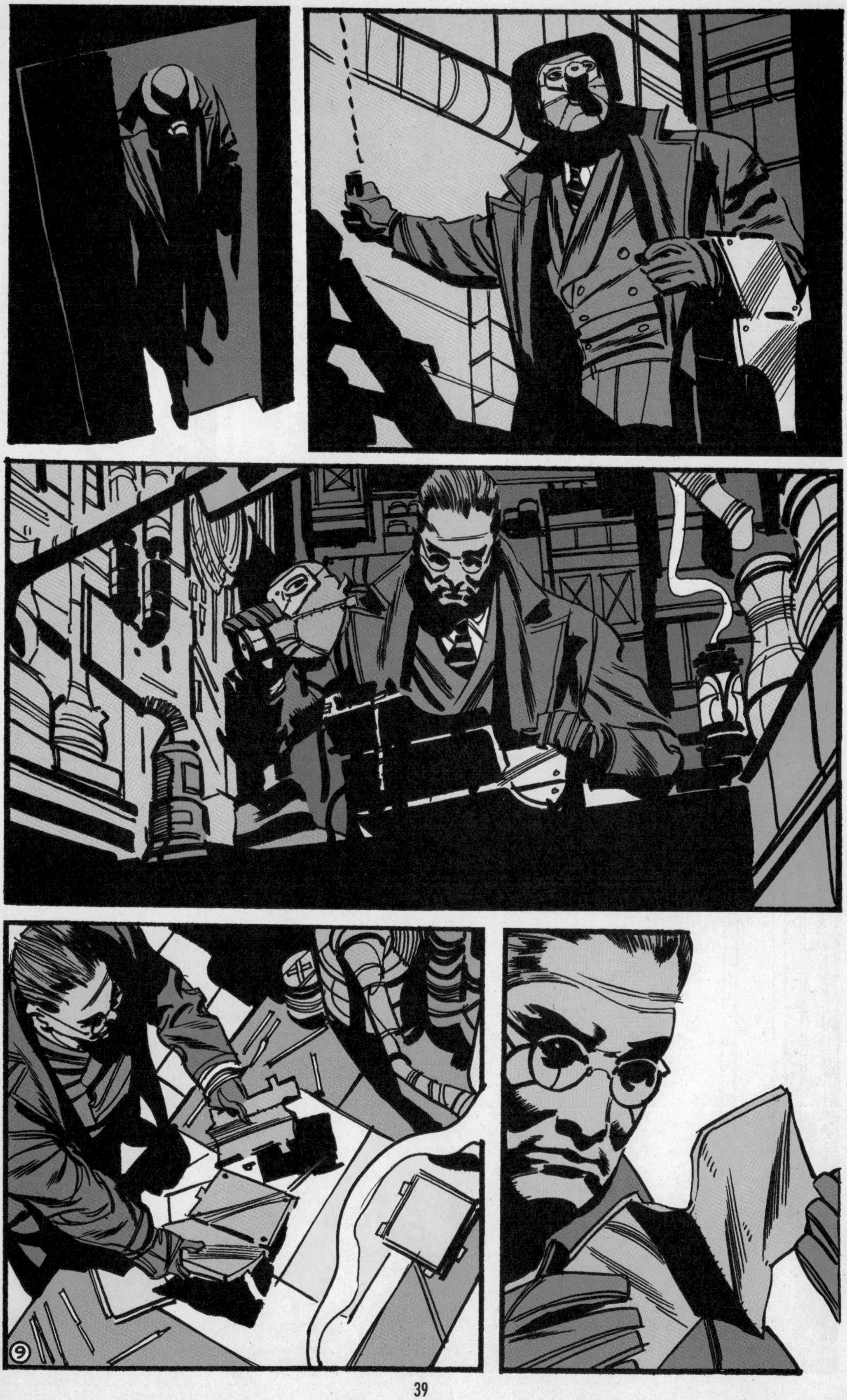
9

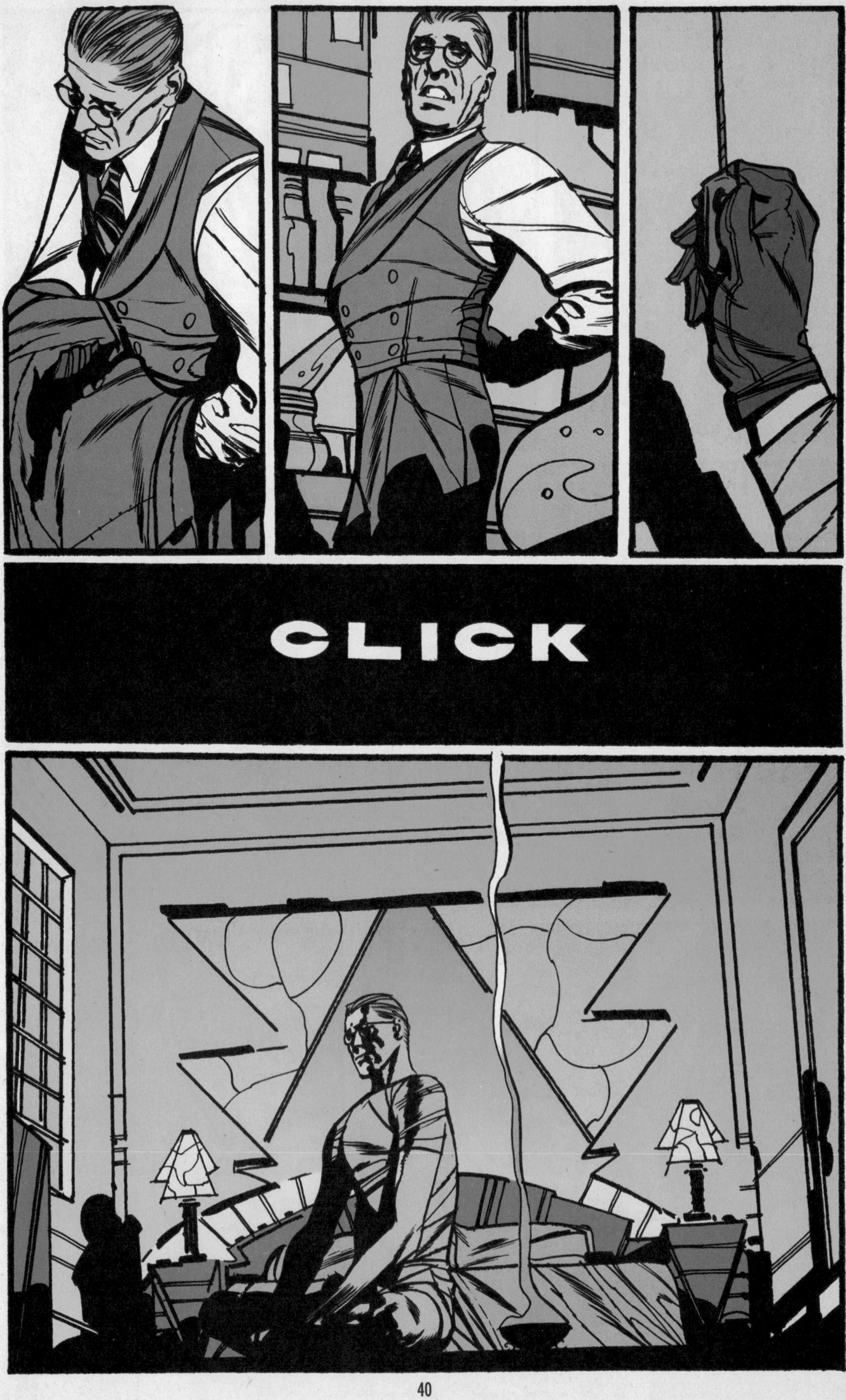
CLICK

LARRY, IRVING... I'VE CALLED YOU HERE TONIGHT TO TALK ABOUT THIS SITUATION IN CHINATOWN.

THIS THING'S A POWDER KEG, AND I WANT IT CORKED.

YOU GOT IT, MR. MAYOR.

I DON'T NEED THIS SHIT RIGHT NOW, SO... COMMISSIONER DAVIS, I WANT THREE TIMES THE POLICE PRESENCE ON THE STREETS IMMEDIATELY.

HAUL IN ANYONE SUSPECTED OF TONG ACTIVITY.

AND, DISTRICT ATTORNEY, I NEED YOU TO MAKE AT LEAST SOME OF THESE CHARGES STICK. AND HURT.

I MUST SAY, YOU SEEM RATHER QUIET ABOUT THE WHOLE MESS.

WASN'T IT YOUR DAUGHTER WHO FOUND THAT GODDAMN HEAD?

YES, SIMPLY BARBARIC.

I JUST FIND THE ENTIRE AFFAIR SUCH A PATHETIC NUISANCE. IF THESE PEOPLE INSIST ON CUTTING EACH OTHER TO RIBBONS...

...WHY DON'T THEY JUST STAY IN THEIR OWN DAMN COUNTRY?

⑪

41

PERSONALLY, I DON'T GIVE A DAMN ABOUT ANYBODY'S INTERNAL STRIFE. I JUST DON'T WANT ANY BLOOD IN MY STREETS.

NO MATTER *WHO'S* DOIN' THE BLEEDIN'.

LIKE THE ITALIANS AND THE IRISH? WE'RE A NATION OF IMMIGRANTS, LARRY.

NEED I POINT OUT THAT THIS SORT OF CIVIL UNREST LOOKS BAD FOR ALL OF US?

ESPECIALLY *YOU,* WHO'S UP FOR RE-ELECTION NEXT YEAR.

VERY WE— THEN.

COMMISSIONER--

--YOU JUST GET THEM BEHIND BARS AND MY OFFICE WILL DO ALL IT CAN TO KEEP THEM THERE. NO MATTER WHAT IT TAKES.

GOOD ENOUGH.

GENTLEMEN... IT'S NICE TO SEE WE'RE ALL IN AGREEMENT ON THIS. NOW, WILL YOU BOTH JOIN ME FOR A WHISKEY?

12

HELLO, JIMMY. IT'S DIAN. I'M... SORRY TO BE CALLING SO LATE.

I HOPE I DIDN'T WAKE YOU.

NOT AT ALL, DIAN. I HAD SOME LATE BUSINESS THIS EVENING.

BUT THIS MAKES TWICE IN ONE DAY THAT WE SPEAK.

I'M GETTING SPOILED.

WELL THEN, HOW'S THIS? I'M CALLING TO SEE IF WE CAN RE-ARRANGE OUR DINNER PLANS. HOW'S TOMORROW NIGHT INSTEAD OF FRIDAY? SAY, EIGHT O'CLOCK AT THE WALDORF? MY TREAT.

HA, YOU ARE A TREAT, DIAN.

EIGHT IT IS. AND I'LL BE COUNTING THE HOURS.

DIAN, WH--?

MARVELOUS! I'LL SEE YOU THEN!

OH, HELLO, DADDY. I DIDN'T HEAR YOU COME IN.

I HAD A MEETING WITH THE MAYOR. WHO WERE YOU CALLING THIS LATE AT NIGHT?

OH, JUST MAKING PLANS FOR TOMORROW NIGHT. I HAVE A DATE...

⑬

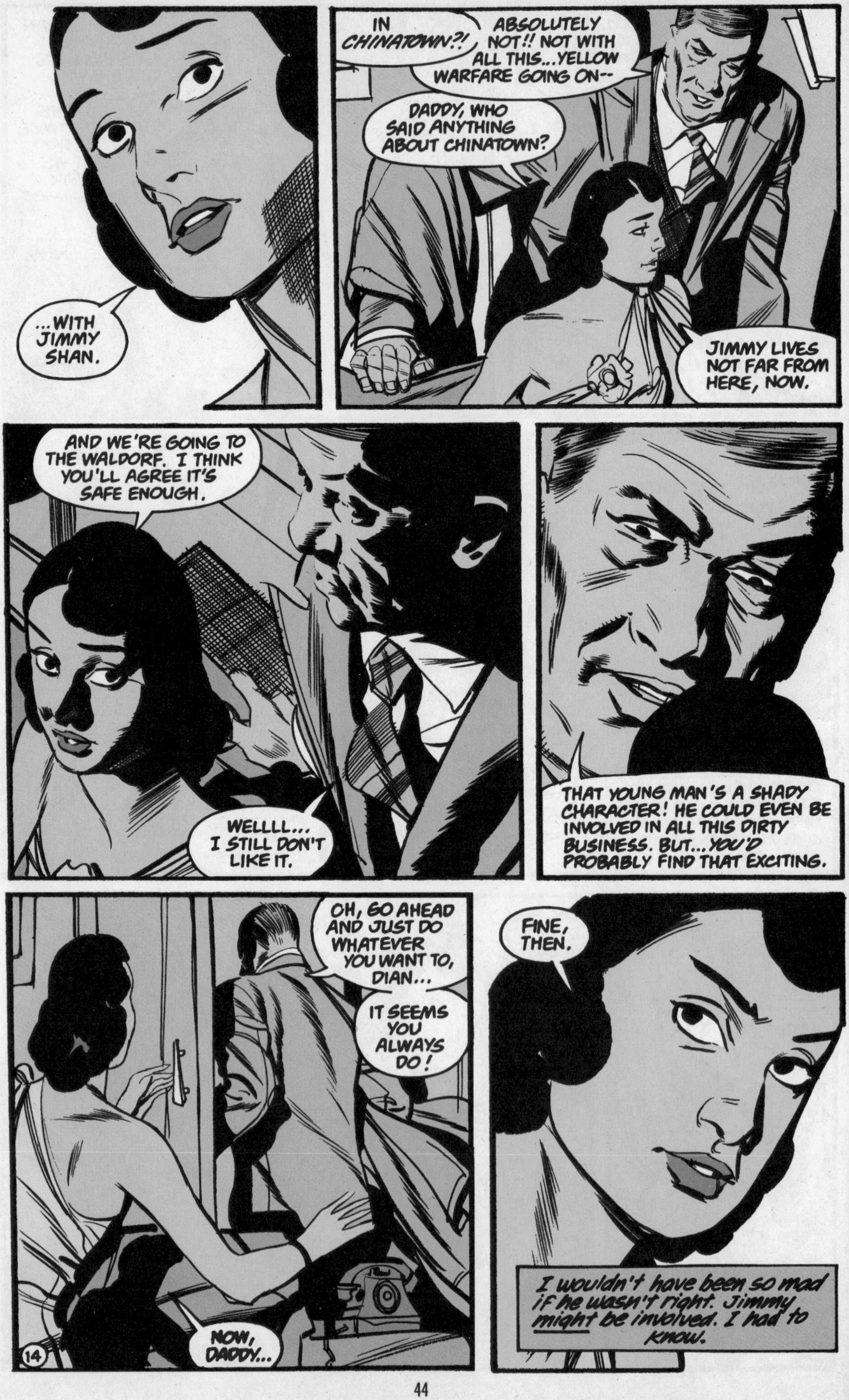
...WITH JIMMY SHAN.
IN CHINATOWN?!
ABSOLUTELY NOT!! NOT WITH ALL THIS...YELLOW WARFARE GOING ON--
DADDY, WHO SAID ANYTHING ABOUT CHINATOWN?
JIMMY LIVES NOT FAR FROM HERE, NOW.
AND WE'RE GOING TO THE WALDORF. I THINK YOU'LL AGREE IT'S SAFE ENOUGH.
WELLLL... I STILL DON'T LIKE IT.
THAT YOUNG MAN'S A SHADY CHARACTER! HE COULD EVEN BE INVOLVED IN ALL THIS DIRTY BUSINESS. BUT...YOU'D PROBABLY FIND THAT EXCITING.
OH, GO AHEAD AND JUST DO WHATEVER YOU WANT TO, DIAN...
IT SEEMS YOU ALWAYS DO!
NOW, DADDY...
14
FINE, THEN.
I wouldn't have been so mad if he wasn't right. Jimmy might be involved. I had to know.

TO DIAN. WHOSE BEAUTY IS MATCHED ONLY BY... WELL, BY NOTHING I CAN THINK OF.

JIMMY... YOU KNOW IT TAKES MORE THAN FLATTERY TO MAKE ME BLUSH. AND CERTAINLY MORE THAN ONE GLASS OF CHAMPAGNE.

SCOUNDREL.

I REMEMBER WHAT MAKES YOU BLUSH... VERY WELL.

WELL, NOW, IF THIS ISN'T A LUCKY COINCIDENCE! GOOD EVENING, DIAN.

JIMMY, MIGHT I STEAL YOU AWAY FOR JUST A MOMENT ...IMPORTANT DETAILS.

MR. ROSS...

WHY, OF COURSE, HERMAN.

DIAN, YOU WON'T MIND?

NO. GO RIGHT AHEAD.

It seemed fate was conspiring to keep me from ever being too close to Jimmy again.

WELL HELLO AGAIN, "STRANGER!"

IT SEEMS THIS REALLY IS BECOMING A HABIT.

WESLEY! WH-WHAT DO YOU MEAN BY THAT?

15

45

WHY, OUR RUNNING INTO EACH OTHER, OF COURSE.

OH! YES...YES, IT CERTAINLY IS. WHAT ARE YOU DOING HERE TONIGHT?

ON A DATE?

NA. NOT ON MY SCHEDULE.

NO, I'M MEETING AN OLD COLLEAGUE OF MY FATHER'S FOR DINNER. HE'S A PROFESSOR OF EASTERN STUDIES AT COLUMBIA AND GIVES ME ADVICE ON OUR FOREIGN MARKETS FROM TIME TO TIME. YOU?

WELL, I AM ON A DA--SPEAK OF THE DEVIL!

JIMMY SHAN... WESLEY DODDS.

I BELIEVE WE'VE MET BEFORE...?

ALMOST. BUT I DON'T WISH TO INTRUDE. I'LL LEAVE YOU BOTH TO ENJOY YOUR EVENING.

GOOD NIGHT, ALL.

SERIOUS FELLOW.

HE CAN BE.

SORRY TO ABANDON YOU LIKE THAT. I KNOW HERMAN CAN BE RATHER ABRUPT.

OH, THAT'S ALL RIGHT. JUST SO LONG AS YOU'RE REALLY MINE FOR THE REST OF THE NIGHT.

FOR AS LONG AS YOU LIKE. UNTIL TOMORROW, EVEN.

WE'LL SEE ABOUT THAT...

16

46

EXTRA! EXTRA!

GETCHA PAPAH! NIGHT-OWL DISHUN! GETCHA PAPUH!

AH TAKE WUN.

HEAH, HEAH, AH SAY AH TAKE WUN.

EXTRA! EXTRA!

BLOW, BO. YOU JINXIN' ALL MY BIZNESS, SCRAM!

AH SAED AH WAN A PAPUH! HEAH D'MONEY.

MAN, GET D-FUH-- YYAAH!

GIVE THE MAN HIS PAPER, BOY.

AND YOU KEEP YOUR ASS AWAY FROM HERE, TOM.

17

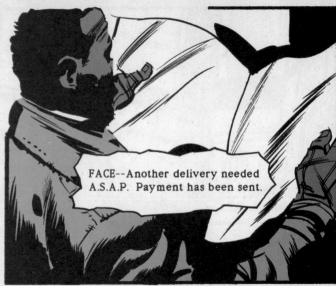

FACE--Another delivery needed A.S.A.P. Payment has been sent.

LOOKIN' FOR A DATE, EH?

HATE TO SAY IT, JUNIOR, BUT I ONLY DO HEAD.

ONE FOR FRENCH. THREE FOR GREEK.

OH, IT'S YOU. THE ROWDY ONE WITH HIS BIG STRONG ROPES.

IT'S 'CAUSE OF YOU, I'M ON MY KNEES THESE DAYS, BUSTER! WELL, I AIN'T OPEN FOR Y--

HEY.

HEY, BACK OFF!! I--

THIS ONE'S ON SOMEONE ELSE'S TAB.

18

At dinner, Jimmy managed to avoid any attempt I made at digging for dirt on the Tongs. Still, frustrated as I was, there's just no denying that charm sometimes.

HIS SENSE OF PLEASURE IS SO INFECTIOUS.

THANKS, JIMMY. THAT WAS REALLY DELIGHTFUL.

IT'S THE DELIGHT I FEEL FROM SEEING YOU AGAIN. AND I...I WISH IT DIDN'T HAVE TO END HERE.

JIMMY, I...

EVENINGS WITH YOU WERE ALWAYS MAGICAL, DIAN. I MISS YOUR FRAGRANCE. YOUR SKIN.

OKAY.

HUH?!

EXCUSE M-- SAY!!

DIAN! WHAT--WHAT IS THIS?!

GOOD EVENING, SIR. NICE TO SEE YOU AGAIN.

SORRY IF WE... DISTURBED YOU.

WHY, YOU...

HER HEADLESS BODY WAS DISCOVERED AN HOUR AGO.

DADDY!

WHAT IS IT? WHAT'S *WRONG?!* WHY ARE YOU RUSHING OUT AT THIS LATE HOUR OF NIGHT?

HMM...? WHY, THERE'S BEEN ANOTHER TONG KILLING, THAT'S WHY. THIS TIME IT WAS A PROSTITUTE.

I DO HOPE YOU PLAN ON STAYING HOME NOW TONIGHT...

ALONE.

WISE ADVICE -- AS WELL AS MY CUE TO SAY, "GOOD NIGHT." I'LL CALL YOU SOON, DIAN.

THE ARGUMENT THAT I KNOW IS COMING CAN JUST WAIT UNTIL TOMORROW. I AM IN A HURRY.

NEED TO TUCK ME IN TOO, DADDY?

BE SERIOUS, DIAN, AND LOCK THE DOOR.

MEN.

20

50

‹CLOSE THE DOOR SMOOTHLY, ZHANG CHAI LAO. THIS ONE WOULD SPEAK TO YOU IN PRIVATE.›

‹WH-WHO ARE YOU?›

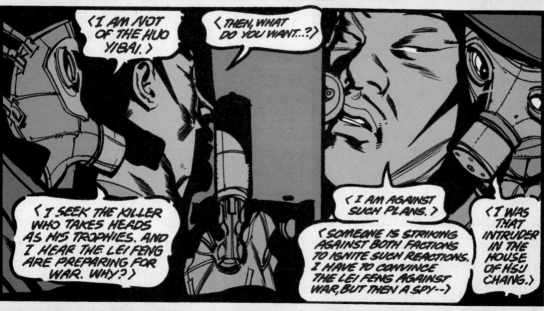

‹I AM NOT OF THE HUO YIBAI.›

‹THEN, WHAT DO YOU WANT...?›

‹I SEEK THE KILLER WHO TAKES HEADS AS HIS TROPHIES. AND I HEAR THE LEI FENG ARE PREPARING FOR WAR. WHY?›

‹I AM AGAINST SUCH PLANS.›

‹SOMEONE IS STRIKING AGAINST BOTH FACTIONS TO IGNITE SUCH REACTIONS. I HAVE TO CONVINCE THE LEI FENG AGAINST WAR, BUT THEN A SPY--›

‹I WAS THAT INTRUDER IN THE HOUSE OF HSÜ CHANG.›

‹BUT WHY DO YOU SEEK THIS KILLER?›

‹TO CAST HIM INTO THE VEIL OF SHADOWS--WHERE HIS OWN FOUL APPETITES WILL CONSUME HIM.›

‹TELL YOUR ELDERS THAT THE SANDMAN HUNTS THIS BEAST WHO PREYS UPON THEM. TO FIGHT AMONGST THEMSELVES IS SHEER SUICIDE.›

‹FOR NONE CAN ESCAPE THE SANDMAN'S DARK DREAM.›

21

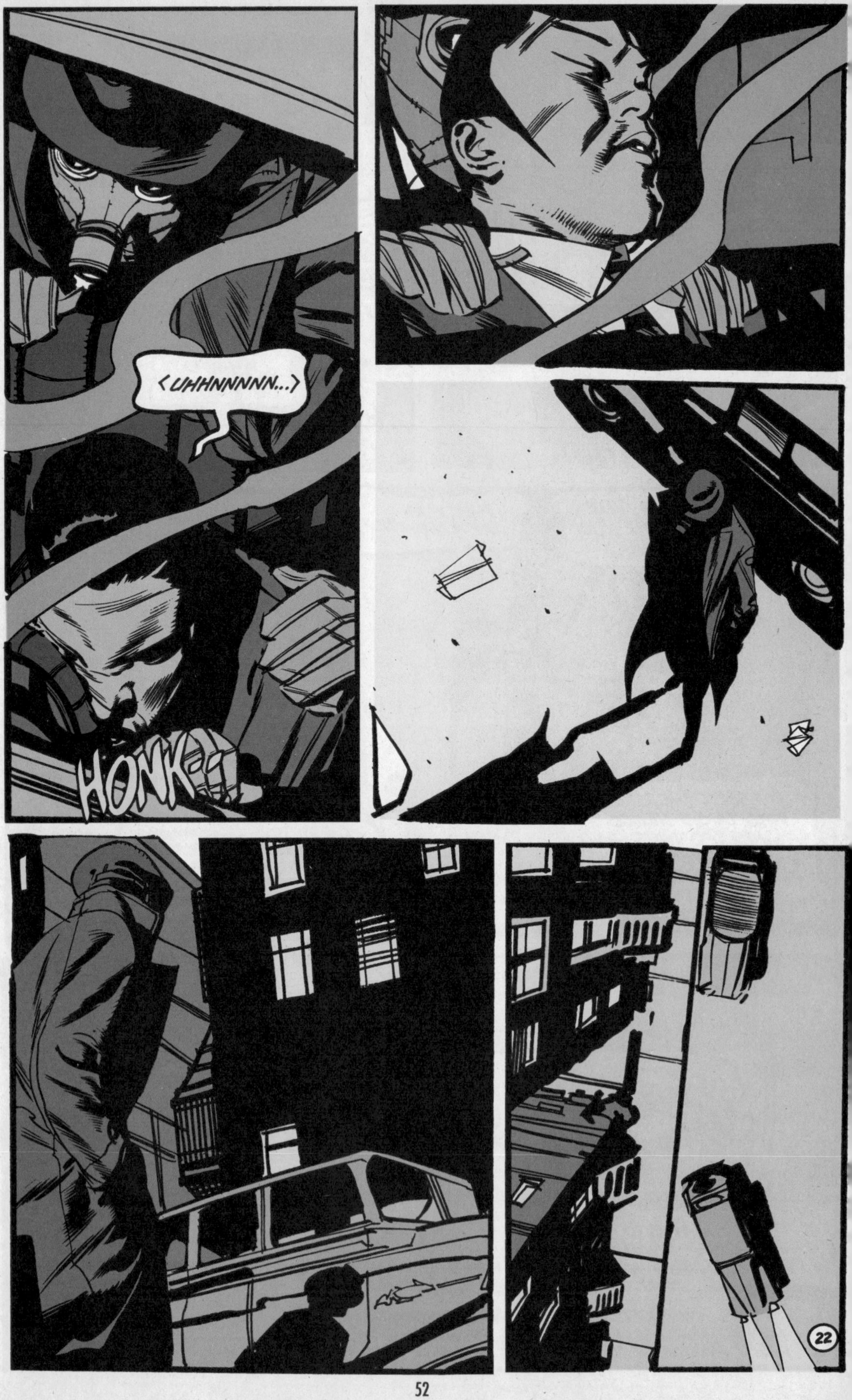

<UHHNNNNN...>
HONK
22

WELL NOW, WELL NOW BEAUTIFUL...

...THAT SHOULD BE THE LAST ONE FOR A WHILE.

MEANS WE CAN FINALLY DITCH THIS SHIT-HOLE.

MOVE BACK HOME AGAIN.

OH, YES, SWEETHEART.

CONGRATULATE YOUR GORGEOUS SELF.

NOTHING EVER ESCAPES YOU.

23

YOU ARE RELENTLESS.

P-P...MMPH--

POWERFUL!

STWONG!

AND SUCH A PWETTY, PWETTY BOY.

Y-YOUR...

I...

S-S-STEADY, NOW SWEETHEART...

NUFFIN' TO WOSE YOUR WITTLE HEAD ABOUT...

OH, NO, NO, NO...

NO INDEED.

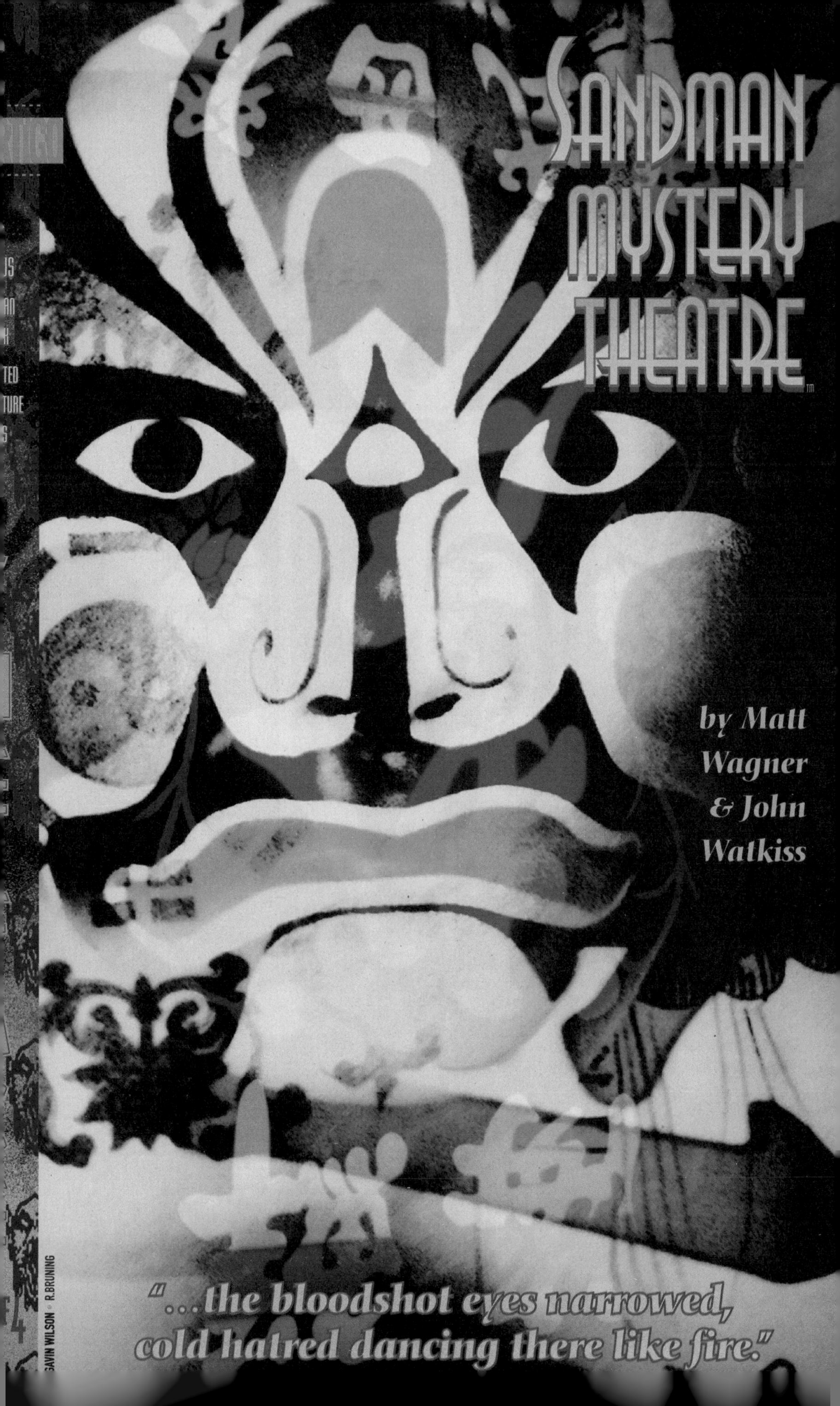
SANDMAN MYSTERY THEATRE
by Matt Wagner & John Watkiss
"...the bloodshot eyes narrowed, cold hatred dancing there like fire."
GAVIN WILSON • R.BRUNING

HEY!

HEY...

WHO'S THERE?!

AWRIGHT, WISE GUY, HOLD IT RIGHT...

56

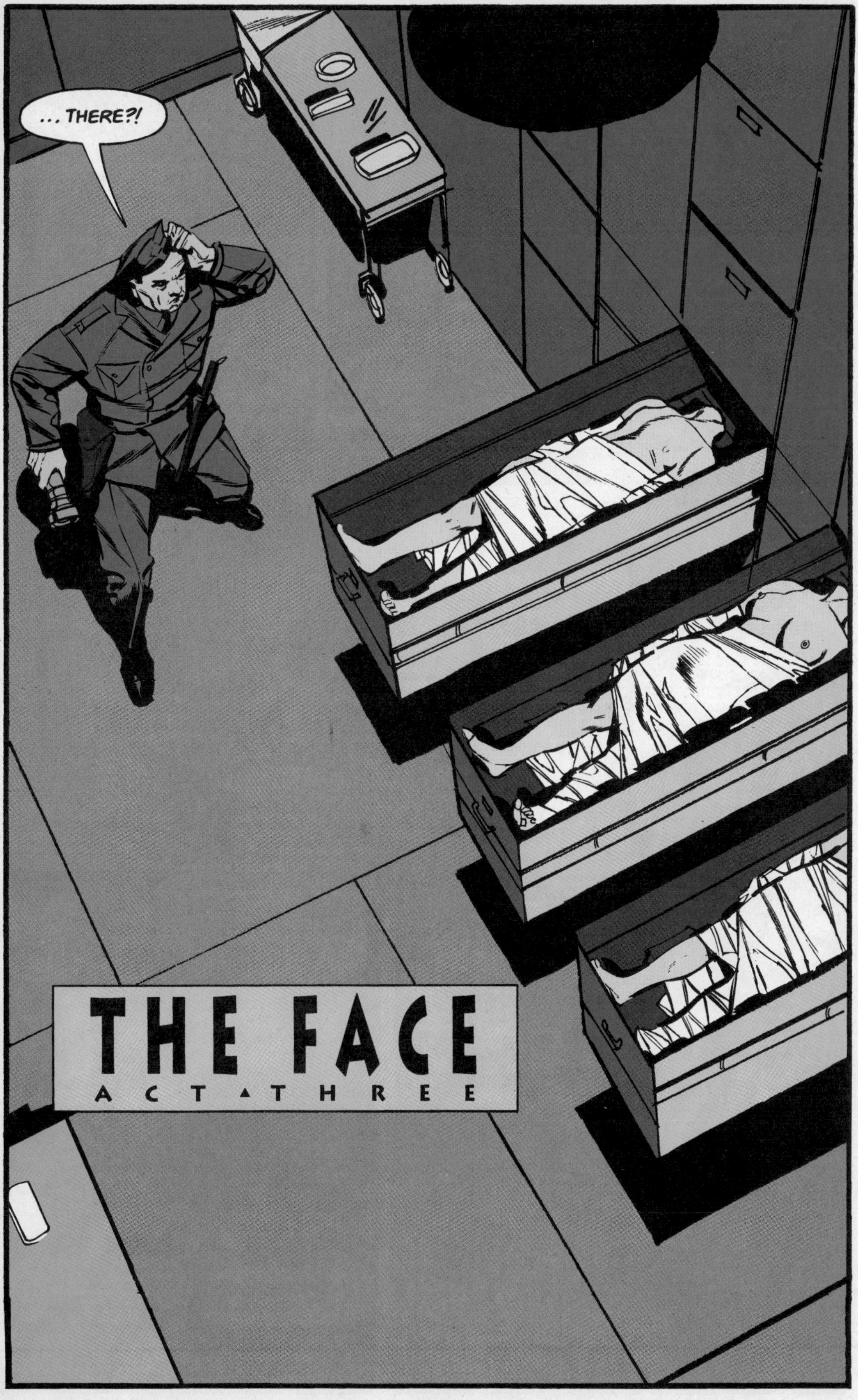
... THERE?!
THE FACE
ACT THREE

TH-DUNK

SKREEEE

⟨UNNH--!
(KOFF, KOFF)⟩

HSSS-- (KOFF,
KOFF) HSSSS--

⟨HSU
CHANG!!⟩

⟨HACK!
(KOFF, KOFF,
KOFF)⟩

⟨OPE-- OPEN UP!
HELLO?! (hack, koff)
OPEN (KOFF, KOFF,
KOFF)⟩

⟨WHAT IS IT?!
WHO DARES
DISTURB THIS
HOUSE...?!⟩

⟨ZHANG CHAI
LAO! WHAT DO
YOU WANT?!⟩

⟨HSU
CHANG!!⟩

⟨KOFF! KOFF!
I MUST BE ALLOWED
TO SPEAK WITH
HSU CHANG! AT
ONCE!⟩

⟨IMPOSSIBLE.
THE HOUR IS--⟩

⟨I BEAR
NEWS OF
THE KILLER!
(KOFF, KOFF)⟩

③

< HONORED HSU CHANG...>

<...EARLIER THIS EVENING I WAS... APPROACHED BY A MAN WHO CLAIMS TO BE THE INTRUDER FOUND IN YOUR HOUSE ON THE EVE OF WAR. A MASKED MAN.>

< HE, TOO, CLAIMS THESE KILLINGS ARE NOT THE WORK OF THE HUO YUBAI. THERE IS A THIRD POWER AT WORK. AN EVIL POWER.>

< HSU CHANS, THIS MAN MADE NO MOVE TO HARM ME, AND HE CLAIMS TO HUNT THIS UNKNOWN KILLER HIMSELF.>

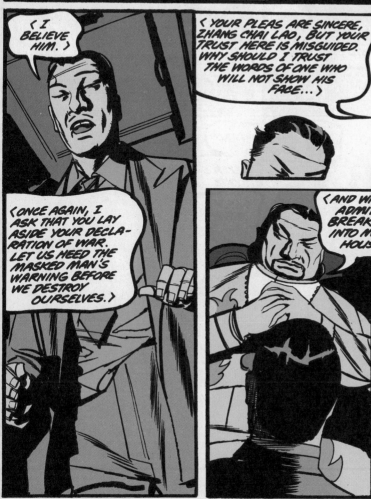

< I BELIEVE HIM.>

< YOUR PLEAS ARE SINCERE, ZHANG CHAI LAO, BUT YOUR TRUST HERE IS MISGUIDED. WHY SHOULD I TRUST THE WORDS OF ONE WHO WILL NOT SHOW HIS FACE...>

< ONCE AGAIN, I ASK THAT YOU LAY ASIDE YOUR DECLA-RATION OF WAR. LET US HEED THE MASKED MAN'S WARNING BEFORE WE DESTROY OURSELVES.>

< AND WHO ADMITS BREAKING INTO MY HOUSE?>

< MUST THE ENTIRE WORLD BE VIEWED AS OUR ENEMIES?! HAS THE WESTERN WORLD TURNED US ALL INTO SAVAGES?!>

< YOU ARE STILL A YOUNG MAN, ZHANG CHAI. >

< AND AS SUCH, YOU SEE THE WORLD AS IT OUGHT TO BE. THERE WAS ANOTHER MURDER COMMITTED EARLIER THIS EVENING -- >

< A SING-SING GIRL. >

< I KNOW. BUT THAT STILL DOES NOT CONDEMN THE HUO YUBAI. AS I SAID -- >

< AS YOU GROW OLDER, MY FRIEND, YOU WILL LEARN. THE WORLD DOES NOT TURN US INTO SAVAGES. >

< WE DO IT TO OURSELVES. >

AAAAAAA...

< LEI PING! N--OH NO. NO. NO. >

< LITTLE ONE... >

< N-N-NUH-- >

< (sob) PLE...PLEASE EXCUSE THIS ONE'S SHAME... AH--AH-- HONORED...S-S-HSU CHANG... >

5

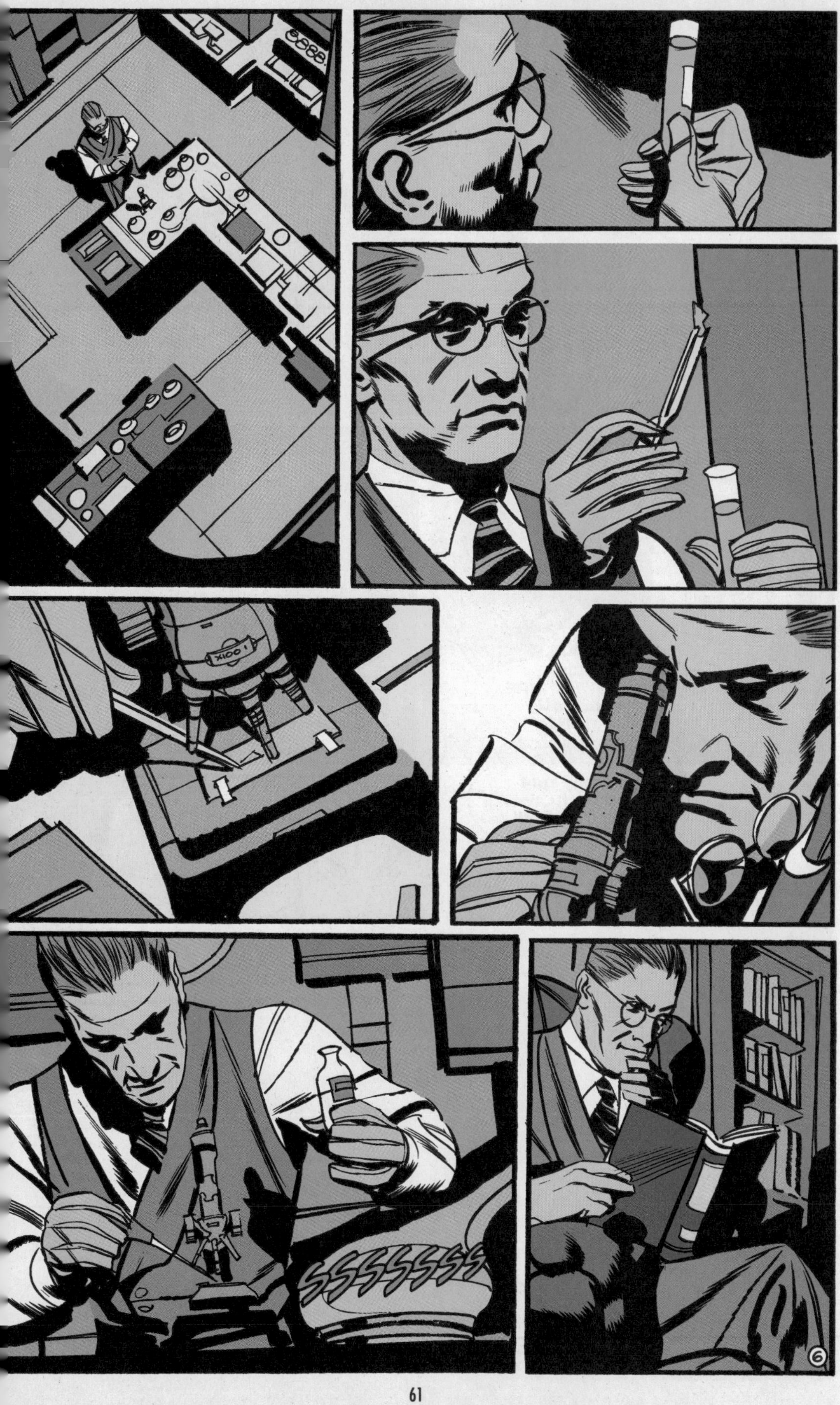
SSSSSSSS
6

BZZZZ

The next day, I had to try to see Jimmy. That scene with Daddy was unforgivable.

WHAT IS IT--?! OH... IT'S YOU.

But things were far worse than I could have imagined.

JIMMY! GOOD LORD, ARE YOU ALL RIGHT? I--I...

MM'FINE, DIAN... JUS' TIRE... WHAT DO YOU WANT?

WELL, I WANTED TO APOLOGIZE... FOR LAST NIGHT'S--

I DON'T CARE ABOUT THAT! DIAN, PLEASE...JUST GO AWAY...

NO! JIMMY, THIS ISN'T LIKE YOU. WHAT'S WRONG?! I KNOW DADDY CAN BE--

DIAN, I SAID I DON'T CARE. COME IN. LEAVE. I DON'T CARE...

JUST LET ME RELAX IN MY PALACE.

MY BIG, GODDAMN ICE PALACE.

AND HERE COMES THE SNOW QUEEN, NOW.

⑦

OH, STOP ALL THIS PIOUS SHIT, JIMMY!

YOU WERE ALWAYS SO PROUD OF THIS APARTMENT. NOW, WHAT IS WRONG WITH YOU?!

EVERYTHING.

I'M THE WRONG SORT OF COLOR. THE WRONG SORT OF CLASS. THE WRONG SORT OF PHILOSOPHY.

WRONG SORT OF SON...

JIMMY, I DON'T UNDERSTAND. THIS ISN'T EVEN ABOUT US? IS IT... IS IT ABOUT THIS SITUATION WITH THE TONG KILLINGS?

THE TONGS!

BAH! BRANDED AS BANDITS FOR SUPPLYING THE LUSTS OF THE WHITE MAN. THE ONLY DECENT LIVING WE ARE ALLOWED IN YOUR WORLD!!

SAY, DON'T MAKE ME PART OF YOUR DRAMATIC SELF-PITY!!

YOUR OPIUM. YOUR GAMBLING. YOUR WHORES... THAT GIRL WHO WAS MURDERED LAST NIGHT...

THAT INNOCENT GIRL...

WELL, I DIDN'T KILL HER!!

THAT GIRL WAS MY SISTER...

8

63

SHE WAS ONLY FIFTEEN.

JIMMY, I...

DIAN, ONCE AGAIN, PLEASE... JUST GO. AND LEAVE ME ALONE.

I...I REALLY WANT TO STAY.

NO.

I didn't wait for the elevator but rather ran down all the stairs. I couldn't bear to pause in my leaving.

If I had looked back I would've drowned along with him.

Drowned in a raging tide of hatreds.

⑨

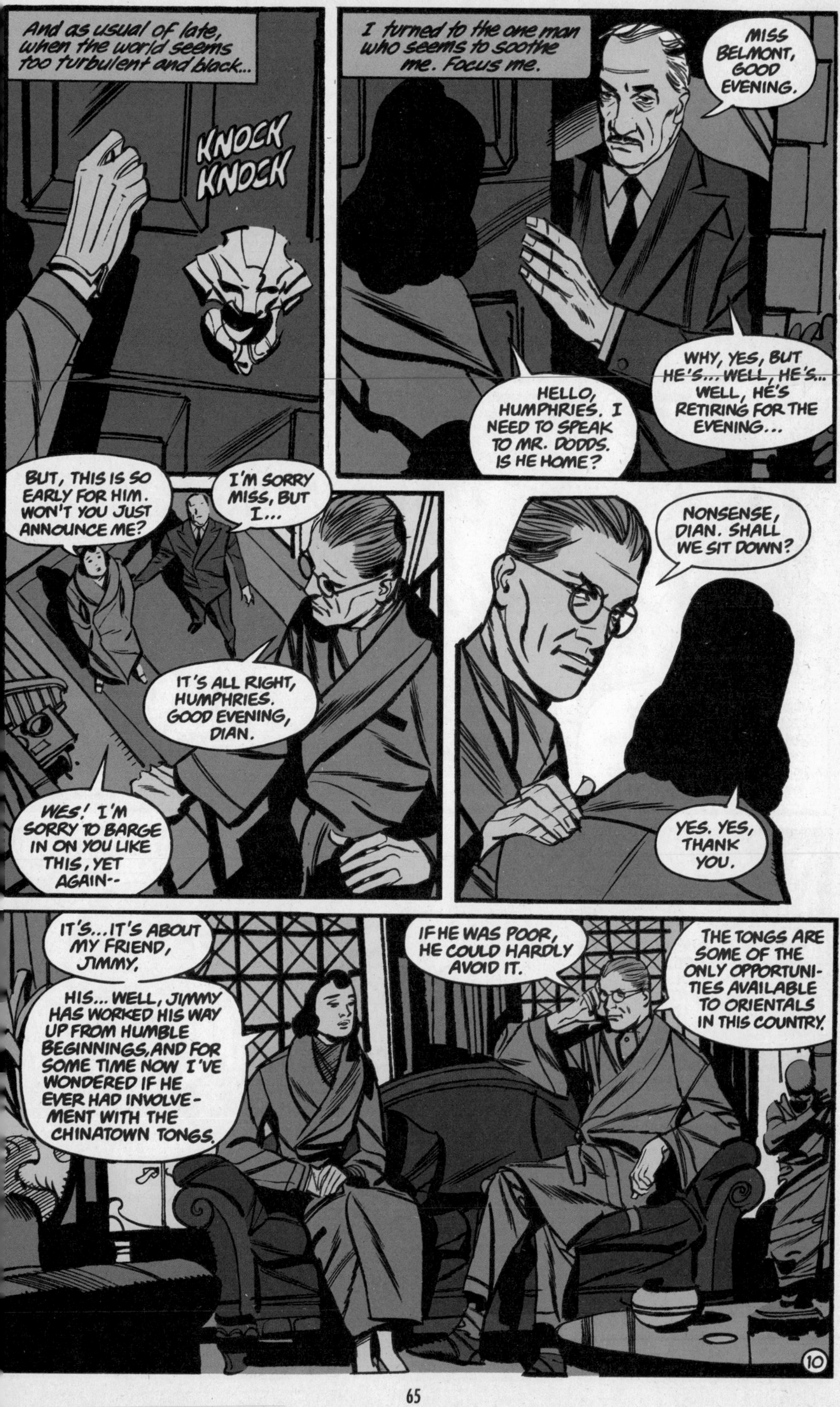
And as usual of late, when the world seems too turbulent and black...
KNOCK KNOCK
I turned to the one man who seems to soothe me. Focus me.
MISS BELMONT, GOOD EVENING.
HELLO, HUMPHRIES. I NEED TO SPEAK TO MR. DODDS. IS HE HOME?
WHY, YES, BUT HE'S... WELL, HE'S... WELL, HE'S RETIRING FOR THE EVENING...
BUT, THIS IS SO EARLY FOR HIM. WON'T YOU JUST ANNOUNCE ME?
I'M SORRY MISS, BUT I...
IT'S ALL RIGHT, HUMPHRIES. GOOD EVENING, DIAN.
WES! I'M SORRY TO BARGE IN ON YOU LIKE THIS, YET AGAIN--
NONSENSE, DIAN. SHALL WE SIT DOWN?
YES. YES, THANK YOU.
IT'S... IT'S ABOUT MY FRIEND, JIMMY,
HIS... WELL, JIMMY HAS WORKED HIS WAY UP FROM HUMBLE BEGINNINGS, AND FOR SOME TIME NOW I'VE WONDERED IF HE EVER HAD INVOLVEMENT WITH THE CHINATOWN TONGS.
IF HE WAS POOR, HE COULD HARDLY AVOID IT.
THE TONGS ARE SOME OF THE ONLY OPPORTUNITIES AVAILABLE TO ORIENTALS IN THIS COUNTRY.
10

GO ON.

WELL, LAST NIGHT THERE WAS ANOTHER MURDER IN CHINATOWN. A YOUNG GIRL. A PROSTITUTE.

SHE WAS JIMMY'S SISTER.

OH, DIAN, I'M SORRY. HOW'S HE HOLDING UP?

NOT SO WELL. BUT HE AS MUCH AS ADMITTED TO ME THAT HE WAS ACTIVE IN THE TONGS. CURRENTLY, IT SEEMED.

YOU'RE SURE OF THIS?

ALMOST CERTAIN. YOU DON'T UNDERSTAND. I SAW A BITTERNESS IN HIM TONIGHT THAT I HAD NEVER SEEN BEFORE. AND NOT JUST GRIEF. HATRED.

SUDDENLY, I COULD BELIEVE ALL MY FATHER'S SUSPICIONS...

HAVE YOU SPOKEN TO YOUR FATHER YET ABOUT THIS?

I SUPPOSE I MUST. I—I DIDN'T LIKE FACING UP TO THIS FACT BUT NOW I CAN'T IGNORE IT.

A GOOD NIGHT'S SLEEP MIGHT HELP.

MAYBE SO.

THAT'S WHERE I'M HEADED MYSELF. PLEASANT DREAMS, DIAN.

GOOD NIGHT, WES. AND THANKS.

YOUR THINGS, SIR...

OKAY, LET'S GO! OPEN UP! WE KNOW YA LIVE UPSTAIRS!!

POLICE!! OPEN UP!

WHAM WHAM WHAM

MEDICAL SUPPLIES

LET'S GO! THIS IS THE POLICE!

PLEASE, PLEASE!! THE NEIGHBORS-- WE ARE CLOSED!

DETECTIVE BURKE, N.Y.P.D. WE NEED ACCESS TO YOUR SALES RECORDS, SO NOW YOU'RE OPEN.

BUT--

NOTHIN' ON YOU, POPS. THIS IS IN CONNECTION WITH THOSE CHINATOWN MURDERS. FORENSICS SAY A SURGICAL HACKSAW WAS USED IN TWO OF 'EM.

BUT THAT THE GUY USING IT WASN'T A DOCTOR.

WE NEED RECORDS OF ALL YOUR CUSTOMERS WITHOUT A MEDICAL LICENSE.

BUT, YOU, EHHH... HAVE NO WARRANT?

WELL, I COULD JUST KICK THE GODDAMN DOOR IN. BUT MY FOOT KINDA HURTS. I MIGHT GET MAD IF I DID THAT.

NO, NO! IT'S OKAY. HERE, SEE? I'M OPENING IT FOR YOU!

OFFI

HMM... THE LIGHT MUST'VE JUST BURNT OUT. IT WAS WORKING EARLI--

McDANIELS, GET OVER HERE WITH YOUR FLASH.

QUICK ABOUT IT.

⑫

67

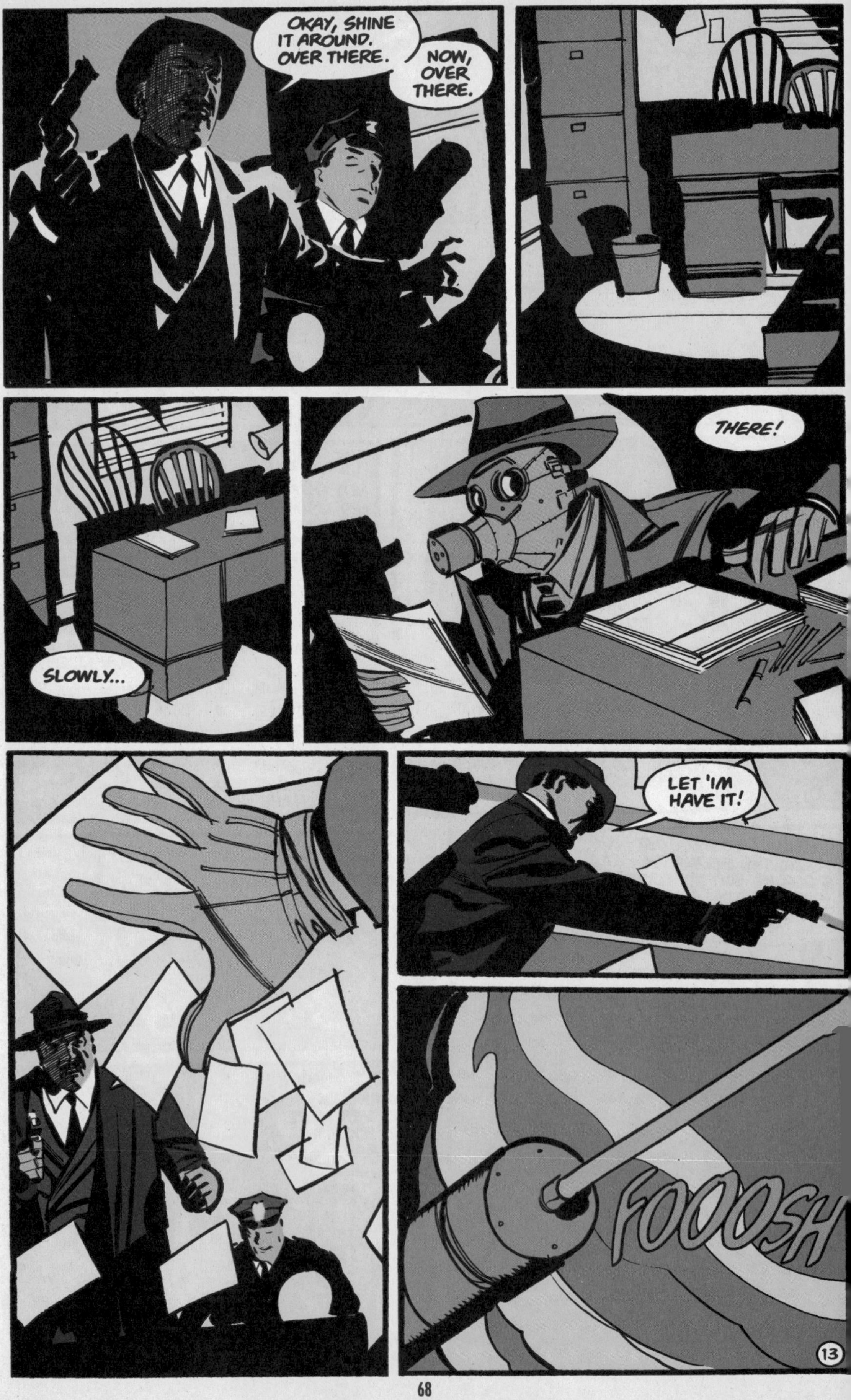

OKAY, SHINE IT AROUND. OVER THERE.
NOW, OVER THERE.
SLOWLY...
THERE!
LET 'IM HAVE IT!
FOOOSH
13

AH--HACK! HACK--! KOFF!

REYNOLDS, WATCH THE DOOR--KOFF-KOFF-KOFF!

<gasp>

COME OUT OF THERE, YOU!

GGAH!

UNNH--

FOOOSH

AACK--!

UNHHH...

<gasp>

<KOFF, KOFF>

MA-- <gasp> MAKES THREE I OWE YOU... BASTARD!! <KOFF, KOFF...>

UNh--

THUD

14

YOU ARE LATE, MR. SHAN.

YES SIR, MR. ROSS.

PLEASE EXCUSE MY TARDINESS. A FAMILY EMERGENCY HAS THROWN ME SOMEWHAT OFF-SCHEDULE.

NOW, BENSON, I'M SURE THE BOY HAS GOOD REASONS. ISN'T THAT RIGHT, JIMMY?

NOW, YOU HAD QUESTIONS REGARDING...?

WHY, THE ANNEX BUILDING WE ALSO DISCUSSED BUYING. HAVE YOU FORGOTTEN WE TALKED ABOUT THIS?

AH YES, OF COURSE...

WELL, I HAVEN'T GOTTEN IN CONTACT WITH THE CURRENT OWNER YET, BUT...

WHEN EXACTLY *WERE* YOU PLANNING ON DOING THIS, JIMMY?

I...APOLOGIZE FOR THIS INCONVENIENCE, GENTLEMEN.

BUT, I WILL RESOLVE THIS POINT IMMEDIATELY. THERE IS *NO PROBLEM* WITH THE STATE OF THINGS ON OUR END, I ASSURE YOU.

AHH... REFRESH MY MEMORY ON THE ADDRESS AGAIN?

15

March 6, 1938 -- the next evening, I tried to confront Daddy with the subject of Jimmy. But I couldn't seem to get his attention away from Fibber and Molly.

NOT THAT CLOSET, McGEE!

AHA-HA-HA-HA-HAAAA!

Or maybe I still wasn't quite convinced enough.

RING RING RING

I'LL-- heh, heh-- I'LL GET IT, DIAN. OH, THAT PROGRAM-- heh...

mdk, mffk. dmrfowmf. safdj slf... WHAT?!

OH, McGEE!!

THE SANDMAN?! THEN HE'S IN ON THE TROUBLE IN CHINATOWN!

GOD-DAMN IT! THE LAST THING WE NEED RIGHT NOW...

"...IS SOMEBODY ELSE STICKING THEIR NOSE INTO THAT MESS."

16

AVERY SHOALS
~ ANTIQUE ~
RESTORATIONS

PLEASANT DREAMS.

FOOSH

YOU ARE AVERY SHOALS?

N–NO.

WHY IS THIS OFFICE AN EMPTY ONE? WHAT SCHEME DOES IT FRONT?

D–DUNNO. JUS' A COURIER.

PICK UP THE MAIL. TAKE 'TA LOCKER AT GRAND CENTRAL.

TELL ME THE NUMBER AND THEN SLEEP.

17

72

FACE: Conference Desired. Tonight at The Metropolitan. Box 32.

SO, I'M HERE, FAT-ASS.

WHAT DO YOU WANT?

WE NEED ANOTHER ONE.

AND NO GIRLS THIS TIME. THOSE SLANTS DON'T GIVE A SHIT ABOUT THEIR WOMEN.

YOUNG MIDTOWN HUSTLER. NAME OF JIMMY SHAN.

MAKE IT HIM.

DIDN'T KNOW YOU LIKED MUSIC, FAT-ASS.

YOU KNOW NOTHING ABOUT ME, FRIEND.

THANK GOD.

MAKE YOUR DEPOSIT, FAT-ASS. BUT THIS WILL BE THE LAST ONE.

18

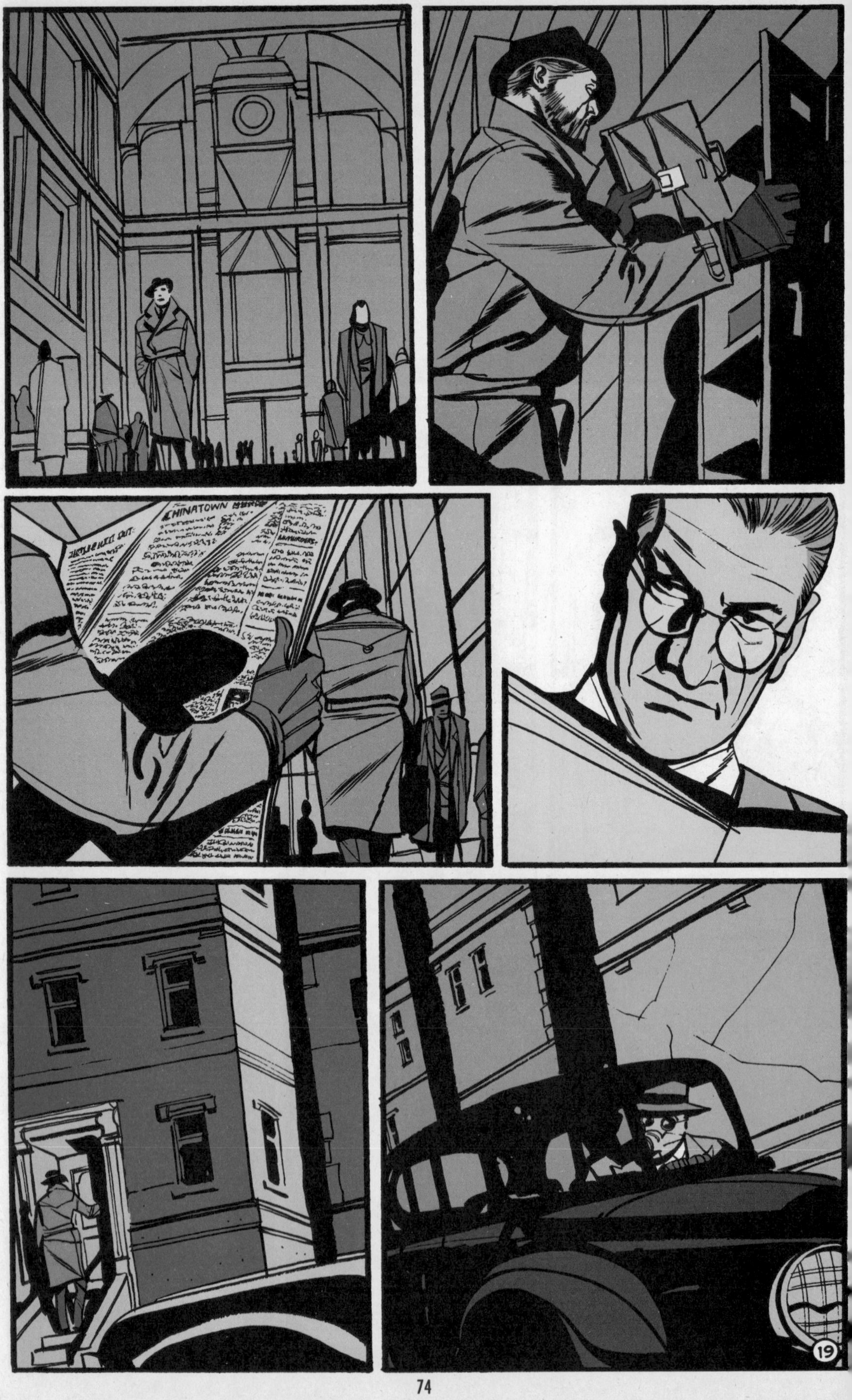
CHINATOWN
19

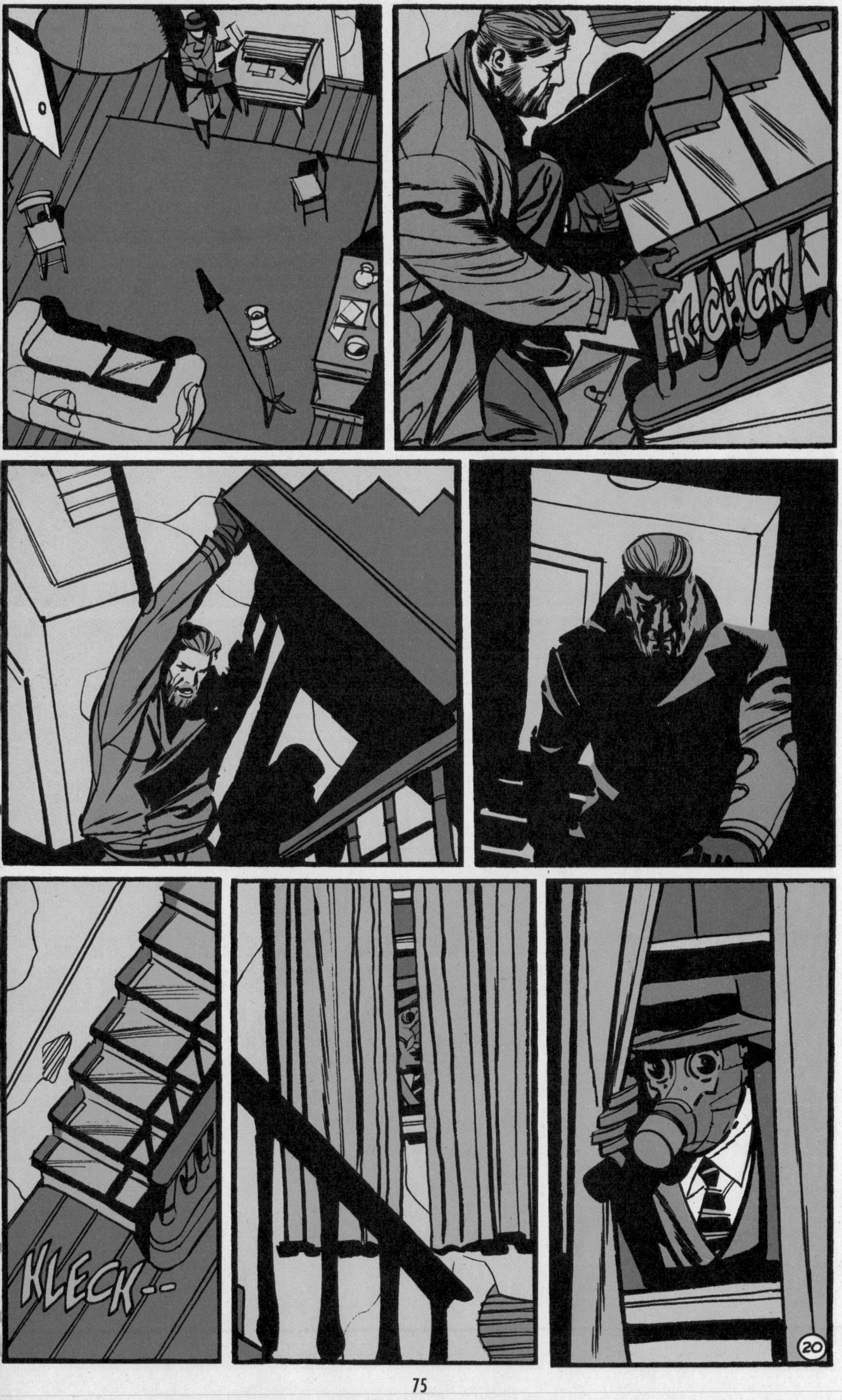
K-CHCK
KLECK--
20

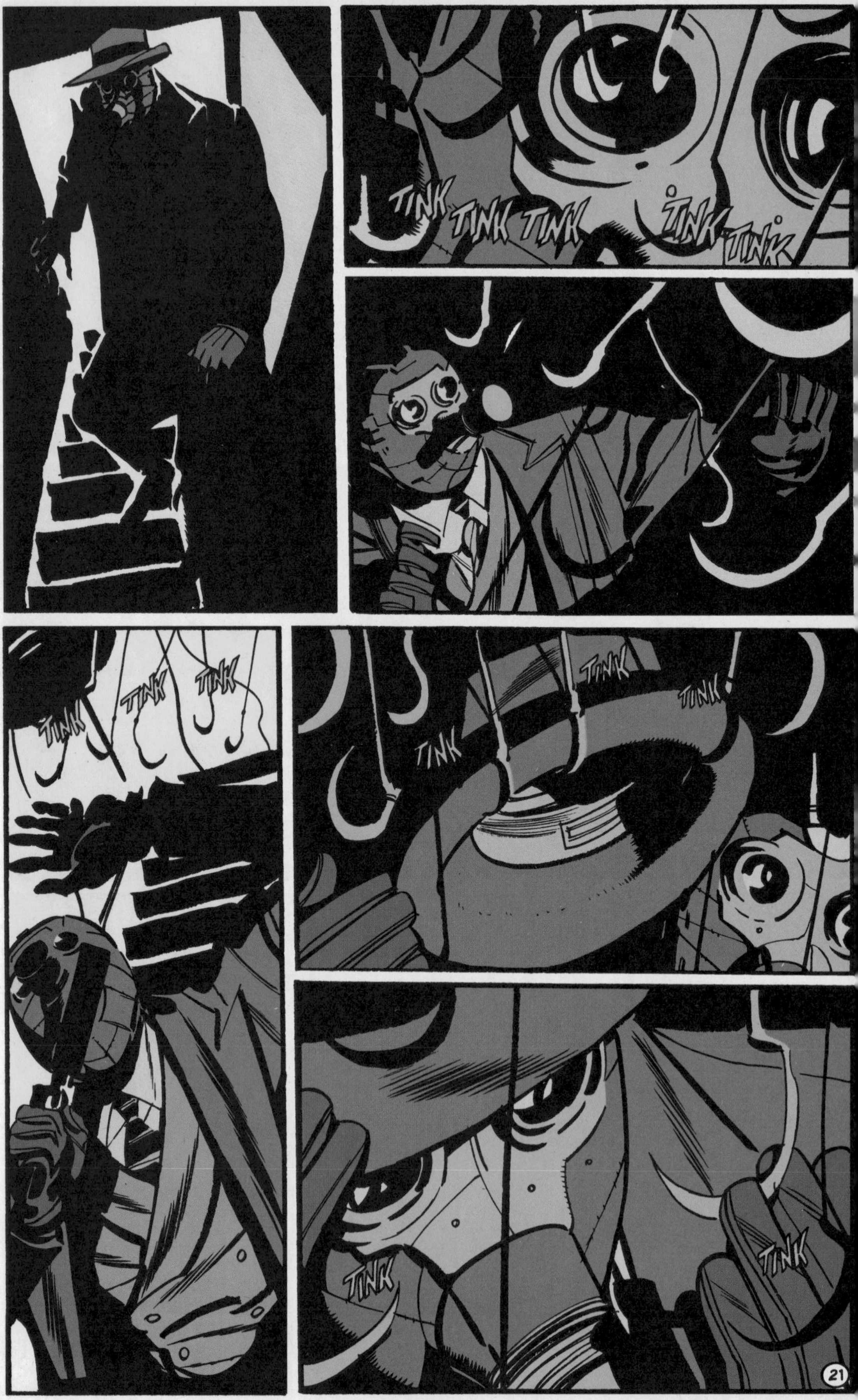
TINK TINK TINK TINK TINK
TINK TINK TINK
TINK TINK TINK
TINK TINK

21

WHAM

22

Oh god, I shake now when I think about it.

What if I hadn't decided to follow him? What if I'd betrayed Jimmy as I'd first intended.

Told Daddy.

I'm still so surprised he never noticed me.

I mean, of course I stood out like a white thumb down there.

In the inner market-places. Where the poverty shows undisguised. Babies in the gutters. Rats every-where.

My God, the things that I saw.

And that Jimmy didn't even seem to notice.

23

78

JIMMY!!

⟨Gasp!⟩

THUNK

OHMIGOD--
JIMMY--

OHMIGOD--

And then I saw blood on his head.

Bright against the shadows and squalor. I don't even remember planning to bring the gun with me.

But, God--Oh, God--thank, God that I did.

JIMMY!!

KRAK

EE-YAAA-GGHHHH!!

OHMIGOD--

DIAN?!

WHAT'RE... GET THE... I--

UNHH...

HELLP!

SOMEBODY! ANYBODY! PLEASE, HELP MEEE...!

DC
VERTIGO

NO. 18
NOV 93
$1.95 US
$2.50 CAN
£1.25 UK
SUGGESTED
FOR MATURE
READERS

THE FACE

2 OF 4

GAVIN WILSON • R.BRUNING

SANDMAN MYSTERY THEATRE

BY MATT WAGNER
& JOHN WATKISS

"...the killer
advanced,
grunting
in rhythm
beneath
the dry,
shiny flesh."

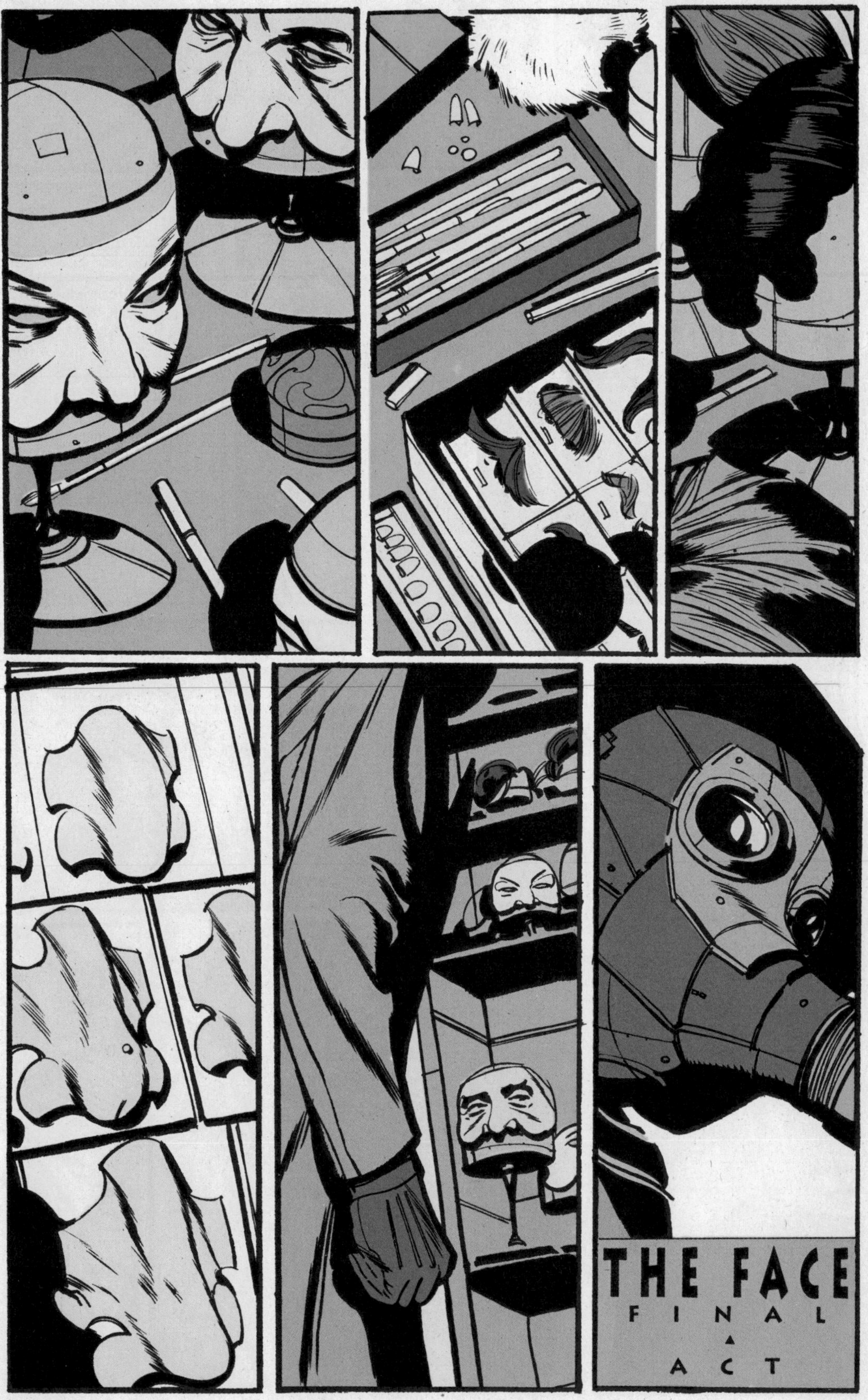
THE FACE
FINAL
ACT

SUPER INDUSTRIAL NOSE-FILTERS

FACE: Conference Desired. Tonight at The Metropolitan. Box 32.

LON CHANEY IN LAUGH OW AU

B-BMP

BMP B-BMP

②

It must've looked strange to those who answered my cries for help--a white woman kneeling over a bleeding Oriental. But to hell with what people thought!

I'M HERE, JIMMY.

DIAN...WHAT-- WHAT HAPPENED? I DON'T REMEMB--

SHHH... JUST RELAX. YOU WERE...YOU WERE ATTACKED.

OH YESSS... I RECALL NOW...

AND THEN... THERE WAS A SHOT.

THAT...THAT WAS ME. I FOLLOWED YOU HERE FROM YOUR APARTMENT. I REALLY DON'T KNOW WHAT I WAS DOING, I...I JUST HAD TO BE SURE YOU WERE--

YOU? YOU FOLLOWED ME?!

JIMMY, THEY SAID YOU SHOULD LIE STILL.

DIAN, SHUT UP! AM I SOME CHILD FOR YOU TO LOOK AFTER?!

3

I DON'T NEED TO BE PROTECTED BY *WOMEN*, DIAN!! OR DID PAPA BELMONT FINALLY WIN HIS CASE? WERE YOU-- *NNGHH*-- WERE YOU SPYING AFTER THE YELLOW MAN'S DIRTY SECRETS?

JIMMY, NO! I--

"JIMMY." *HA!!* YOU DON'T EVEN REMEMBER MY REAL NAME, DO YOU? JUST GET THE HELL AWAY FROM ME, SNOW QUEEN.

I ALWAYS KNEW YOU WERE ONLY SLUMMING.

OH, JIMMY...

ALL RIGHT, YOUNG LADY, THIS... THIS *BULLSHIT* HAS GONE ON LONG ENOUGH!

DADDY!!

4

BMP
B-BMP
BMP
BMP

SSSHHHH IN
CHANEY
"LAUGH
CLOWN
LAUGH"

NNNGHH...
EEE! EEE!
EEE!

KLMP
KLMP
KLMP

YYYAAGGHH...

OH--OH,
SWEETHEART...
EEE!...
NNNGGH--

WH-- WHAT
HAVE THEY DONE
TO US, BABY?!

NNNGGH--

EEE!

LON
CHANEY
IN
"LAUGH
CLOWN
LAUGH"

THEY-- SHE...
SHE SHOT OUR
GORGEOUS BODY...
OUR...BEAUTIFUL...

...POWERFUL...

...BODY--
EH?!

YOU ARE IN PAIN.
PLEASANT D--

5

85

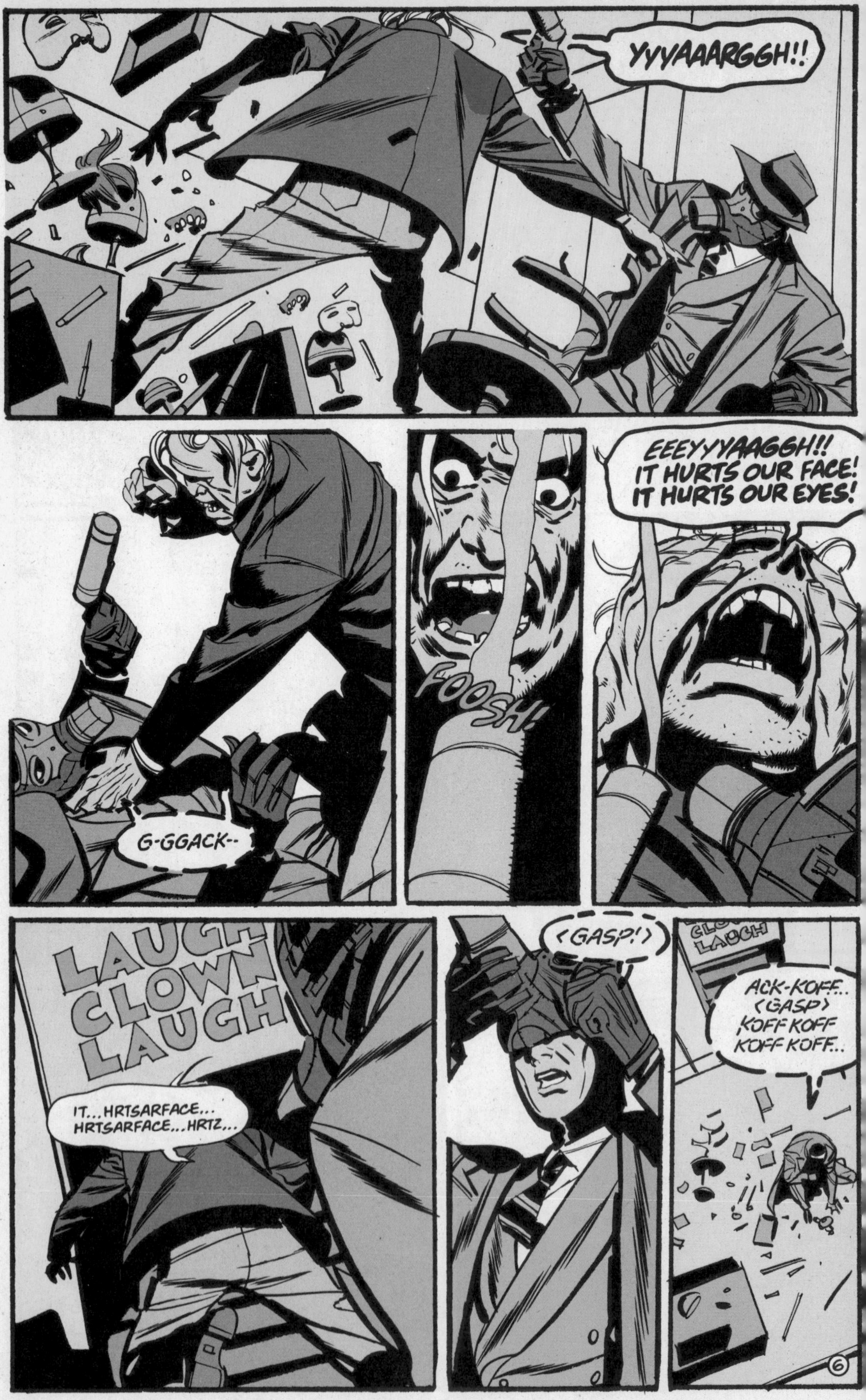
YYYAAARGGH!!
G-GGACK--
FOOSH!
EEEYYYAAGGH!!
IT HURTS OUR FACE!
IT HURTS OUR EYES!
LAUGH CLOWN LAUGH
IT...HRTSARFACE...
HRTSARFACE...HRTZ...
<GASP!>
CLOWN LAUGH
ACK-KOFF...
<GASP>
KOFF KOFF
KOFF KOFF...
6

I had refused to speak to Daddy all the long, dark ride home. That situation soon changed once we were inside the door.

AND, FURTHER-MORE...

I AM NOT A CHILD!!

HE'D HAVE BEEN *KILLED* IF NOT FOR ME!

AND GOOD RIDDANCE.

THE VERY FACT OF HIS ASSAULT POINTS TO HOW DEEPLY HE MUST BE INVOLVED! THAT DIRTY, LITTLE, YELLOW BASTARD...

DADDY!!

I MEAN IT! JUST LOOK AT WHAT HIS INFLUENCE HAS DONE TO YOU, DIAN!

SNEAKING AROUND IN THE NIGHT, *STEALING* MY REVOLVER TO TAKE WITH YOU...

WHICH *YOU* INSISTED I LEARN HOW TO USE!

YES, BUT TO PROTECT YOURSELF. *NOT* TO TAKE THE LAW INTO YOUR OWN HANDS!!

LIKE SOME...SOME VIGILANTE DEBUTANTE!!

OH, DADDY, COME ON...

⑦

YOU MAKE IT SOUND LIKE I'M THE "SANDWOMAN."

DIAN, DON'T BE RIDICULOUS. YOU'RE MY DAUGHTER.

NOW, MAYBE IT DOESN'T OCCUR TO YOU HOW THE DISTRICT ATTORNEY'S DAUGHTER BEING INVOLVED IN SUCH AFFAIRS MIGHT PROVE DAMAGING, SO I'M AFRAID I'VE GOT TO PLACE YOU ON HOUSE ARREST.

DADDY, PLEASE, I...YOU...?

WHAT?! WHAT EXACTLY DO YOU MEAN BY THA--

OFFICER?

EVENIN', SIR.

MY DAUGHTER IS TO NEITHER LEAVE THE PREMISES THIS EVENING, NOR TO RECEIVE VISITORS OF ANY SORT. IS THAT CLEAR?

YES SIR.

SLAM!

At first I couldn't believe it.

Locked in my room like some bloody teenager! And I'd be *damned* if I was going to crawl through the goddamn window.

Damn it! Damn it! Damn it!

8

88

OKAY?!

YOU GOT THAT?!

READ IT BACK TO ME!

UH-HUH. RIGHT. YES.

FINE.

NOW, THAT *MUST* RUN IN THIS EVENING'S NIGHT OWL EDITION. IT IS *VERY* IMPORTANT THAT THE PERSON RECEIVE THIS ANNOUNCEMENT.

YEAH, YEAH, GOOD NIGHT, GOOD NIGHT... JESUS!

YOU! I'LL TAKE A DOUBLE SHOT OF WHISKEY. NO! BRING THE BOTTLE.

OKAY! OKAY! CHRIST, YOU'RE HURTING ME!!

WELL, NOW, TALL AND DARK... IS THERE HANDSOME UNDERNEATH THAT COLLAR AS WELL?

LET'S SEE...

CAREFUL, LITTLE GIRLY.

GET TOO CLOSE AND I MIGHT JUST BITE YOUR HEAD OFF.

HEH.

CHEW UP YOUR BRAIN AND SPIT OUT YOUR EYES.

9

WHERE YA HEADED, HONEY?

231.

OH, YEAHHH... THE YELLOW ONE.

I DIDN'T THINK WE TOOK... THEM.

REALLY? I DON'T KNOW THE POLICY. OH WELL, DOESN'T BOTHER ME.

I JUST WISH THEY SPOKE GOOD ENGLISH.

YEAH?

231

MMM. MOST OF THEM ARE KIND OF SIMPLE, I HEAR. BUT, AT LEAST THEY DON'T SMELL BAD LIKE THE COLOREDS.

GOOD LUCK...

THANKS. I'LL...

I'LL...

WHY, TH-THE PATIENT, HE... HE'S GONE!! ESCAPED!

231

⑩

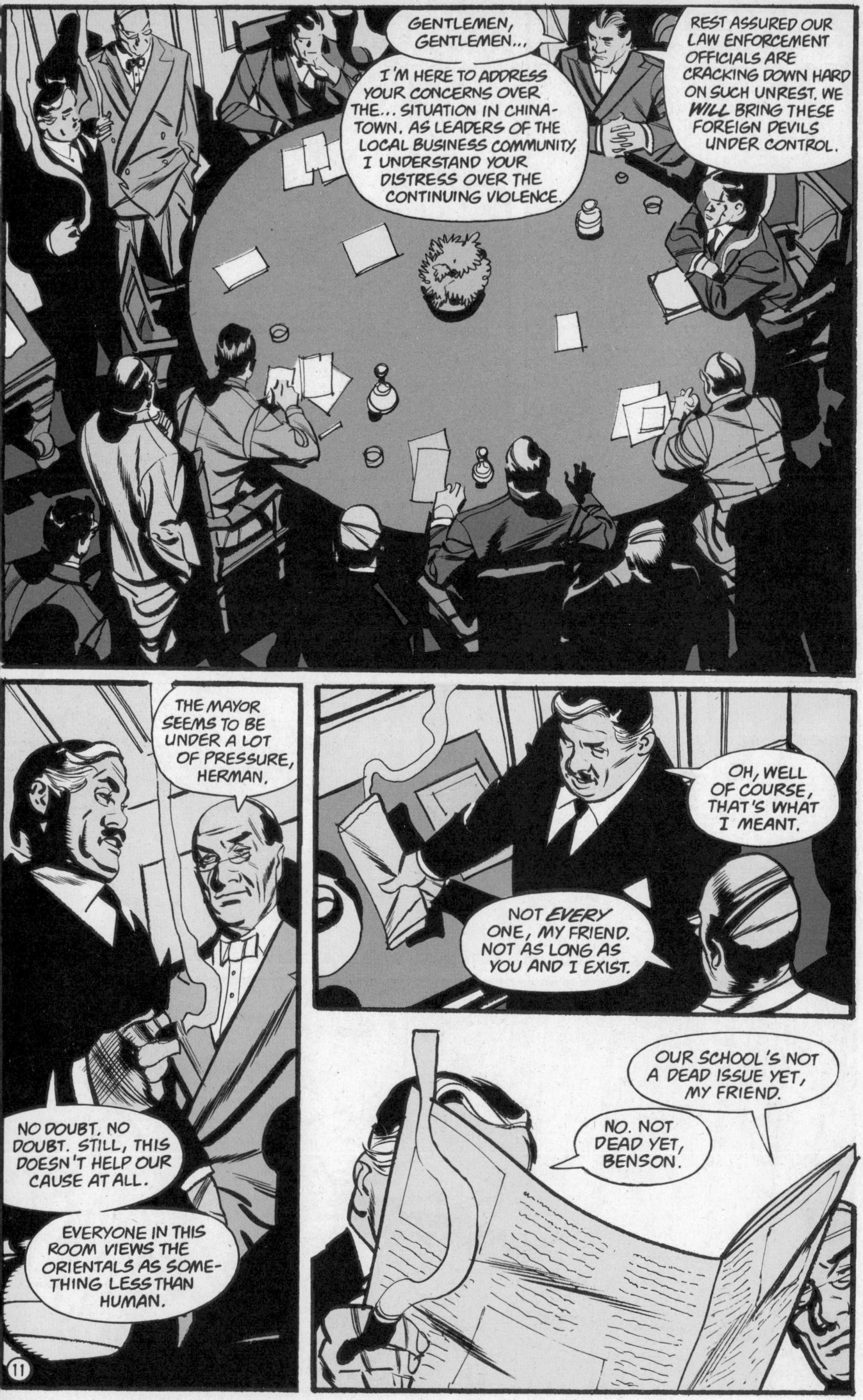
GENTLEMEN, GENTLEMEN...
I'M HERE TO ADDRESS YOUR CONCERNS OVER THE... SITUATION IN CHINA-TOWN. AS LEADERS OF THE LOCAL BUSINESS COMMUNITY, I UNDERSTAND YOUR DISTRESS OVER THE CONTINUING VIOLENCE.
REST ASSURED OUR LAW ENFORCEMENT OFFICIALS ARE CRACKING DOWN HARD ON SUCH UNREST. WE WILL BRING THESE FOREIGN DEVILS UNDER CONTROL.
THE MAYOR SEEMS TO BE UNDER A LOT OF PRESSURE, HERMAN.
OH, WELL OF COURSE, THAT'S WHAT I MEANT.
NOT EVERY ONE, MY FRIEND. NOT AS LONG AS YOU AND I EXIST.
NO DOUBT, NO DOUBT. STILL, THIS DOESN'T HELP OUR CAUSE AT ALL.
EVERYONE IN THIS ROOM VIEWS THE ORIENTALS AS SOME-THING LESS THAN HUMAN.
OUR SCHOOL'S NOT A DEAD ISSUE YET, MY FRIEND.
NO. NOT DEAD YET, BENSON.
11

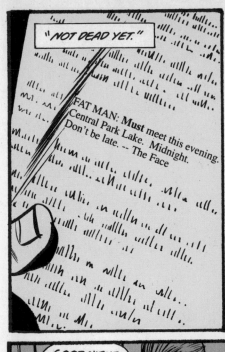

"NOT DEAD YET."

FAT MAN: **Must** meet this evening.
Central Park Lake. Midnight.
Don't be late. -- The Face

GOOD NIGHT, MR. WESLEY DODDS.

AND PLEASANT DREAMS.

⑫

The longer I sat there, stewing inside the confines of my own house, the more sure I became that Jimmy was still in danger.

If only from himself.

HELP!!!

HELP! EEEEEE-- HE'S...HE'S RAISING HIS HANDS TO MY THROAT!! SOMEBODY... ANYONE...PLEASE...

HELP MEEEEEEE--

TUNE IN NEXT WEEK FOR THE EXCITING CONCLUSION TO THIS EPISODE OF...*THE INNER SANCTUM!!*

13

GODDAMN HIM. IT'S TWENTY PAST AND *HE* SAID, "DON'T *BE LATE.*"

DRIVER, CHECK ALONG THAT PATH THROUGH THE TREES. HIM AND HIS GODDAMN GAMES.

YES, SIR.

HE'S LUCKY I EVEN ANSWERED HIS GODDAMN AD. CHRIST, IT'S COLD OUT HERE, TOO.

WELL?!

NOTHING.

HHMMPPH--

WELL, THAT'S IT. LET'S GO, DRIVER. THIS MARKS THE END OF MY INVOLVEMENT WITH THE FACE.

HOW RIGHT YOU ARE, SIR...

⑭

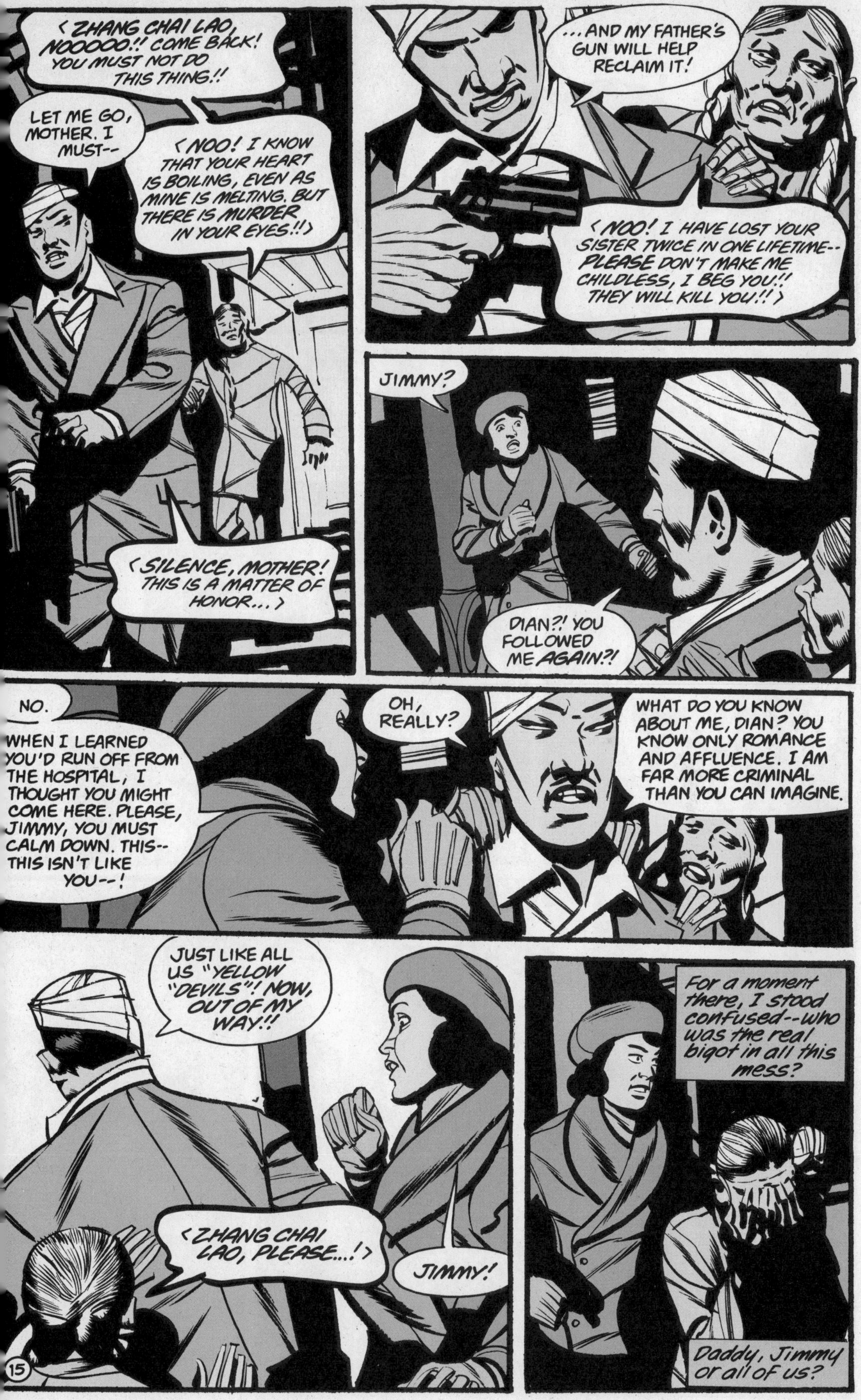

‹ZHANG CHAI LAO, NOOOOO!! COME BACK! YOU MUST NOT DO THIS THING!!›
LET ME GO, MOTHER. I MUST--
‹NOO! I KNOW THAT YOUR HEART IS BOILING, EVEN AS MINE IS MELTING. BUT THERE IS MURDER IN YOUR EYES!!›
‹SILENCE, MOTHER! THIS IS A MATTER OF HONOR...›
...AND MY FATHER'S GUN WILL HELP RECLAIM IT!
‹NOO! I HAVE LOST YOUR SISTER TWICE IN ONE LIFETIME-- PLEASE DON'T MAKE ME CHILDLESS, I BEG YOU!! THEY WILL KILL YOU!!›
JIMMY?
DIAN?! YOU FOLLOWED ME AGAIN?!
NO.
WHEN I LEARNED YOU'D RUN OFF FROM THE HOSPITAL, I THOUGHT YOU MIGHT COME HERE. PLEASE, JIMMY, YOU MUST CALM DOWN. THIS-- THIS ISN'T LIKE YOU--!
OH, REALLY?
WHAT DO YOU KNOW ABOUT ME, DIAN? YOU KNOW ONLY ROMANCE AND AFFLUENCE. I AM FAR MORE CRIMINAL THAN YOU CAN IMAGINE.
JUST LIKE ALL US "YELLOW "DEVILS"! NOW, OUT OF MY WAY!!
‹ZHANG CHAI LAO, PLEASE...!›
JIMMY!
For a moment there, I stood confused--who was the real bigot in all this mess?
Daddy, Jimmy or all of us?

CHAK!!

AAGH!

OH-SWEET-JESUS, IT'S *YOU*...

RIGHT YOU ARE, *FAT-ASS*!!

B-BUT *WHY?!* YOU WERE P-P-PAID--

YOU WEASEL.

YOU SET ME UP! HAD ME FOLLOWED!! ATTACKED!!

WH-WHAT?! *NO!!*

I-I DON'T KNOW WHAT YOU'RE TALKING ABOUT! PL-PLEASE... MY ARM--

SHUT UP, LIAR!!

YOU TRIED TO CLEAN UP YOUR DIRTY LITTLE TRAIL.

16

BUT THEN, MEN LIKE YOU ALWAYS DO.

HMM...?

HEH?

HEH.

HEH. HEH, HA... HEH... HA, HA, HA!

HA! HA! HA!

THE FACE!! BETRAYED BY A MASK!!

I DON'T KNOW WHO YOU ARE NOW, FAT-ASS...

BUT IT DOESN'T REALLY MATTER ANYWA--EH?!!

17

< WU SUNG... MASTER OF THE HUO YUBAI. >

< AUTHOR OF MY SISTER'S DEATH! >

JIMMY...?

I couldn't let him escape me now.

Not with so much left unsaid.

Not with so much hatred walled up between us. Not with his finger on the very trigger of that hatred.

18

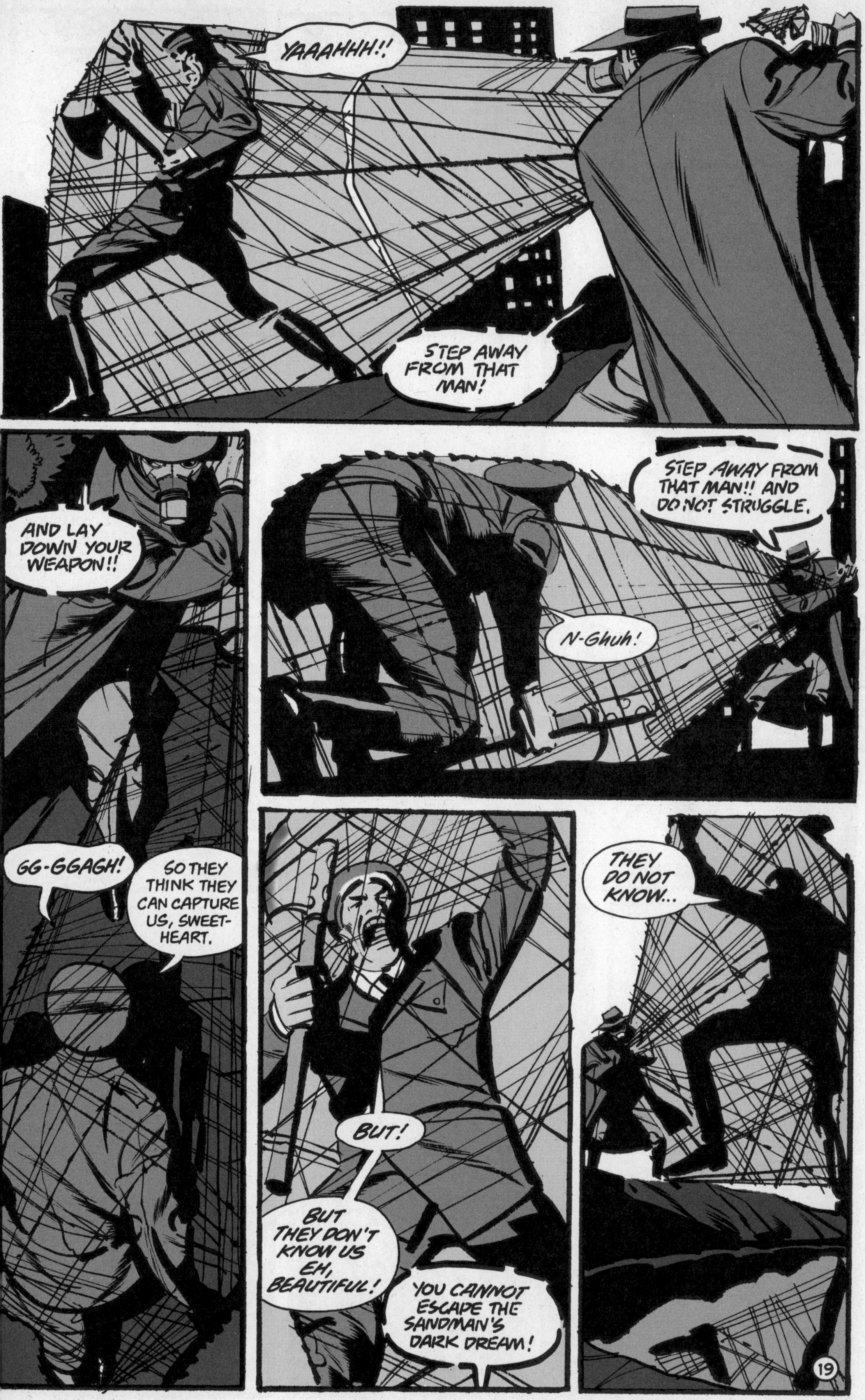
YAAAHHH!!
STEP AWAY FROM THAT MAN!
AND LAY DOWN YOUR WEAPON!!
STEP AWAY FROM THAT MAN!! AND DO NOT STRUGGLE.
N-Ghuh!
GG-GGAGH!
SO THEY THINK THEY CAN CAPTURE US, SWEET-HEART.
BUT!
BUT THEY DON'T KNOW US EH, BEAUTIFUL!
YOU CANNOT ESCAPE THE SANDMAN'S DARK DREAM!
THEY DO NOT KNOW...
19

...OUR ABSOLUTE SPIRIT AND RAGE!! GGHHAA--

SPLAASH!

GLLLGG-- bb-beoofull... blb--

STOP STRUGGLING! I WILL PULL YOU ASHORE--

CHANK!

TH-glb... THEY DON'T KNOW-- Glgg...

...anythigglla-- g--glbb... blb. b...

H-HELP! WH-WHO ARE YOU?!

PL--PLEASE, MY ARM...

FOOSH!

⑳

I AM READY TO DIE!

DIAN, GET OUT OF THE WAY!!

WELL? GO AHEAD. DON'T YOU HATE ME AS WELL AS THE REST OF THE WORLD?

JIMMY, I REFUSE TO BELIEVE YOU REALLY *WANT* THIS!

YOU--YOU'LL HAVE TO SHOOT ME FIRST TO GO THROUGH WITH IT.

JIMMY, NO!!

I...

I...DIAN, I--FEEL LIKE I'M OUT OF MY MIND.

I FEEL LIKE I'M DYING ALREADY...

YOUNG LADY.

STOP THIS INSANITY!! END IT HERE! IT WON'T CHANGE YOUR SISTER'S DEATH! YOU ARE NOT A KILLER!

PLEASE REMOVE YOUR FRIEND, THIS GUTTER TRASH, FROM MY PRESENCE--AT ONCE. OR HE WILL FIND HIS FEELINGS A REALITY!

JIMMY...?

C'MON, THIS WAY. WE'LL TAKE A TAXI BACK TO YOUR PLACE. WE CAN TALK...

NO, DIAN.

NEVER AGAIN.

WE... I... I WANT TO THANK YOU FOR CARING SO DEEPLY.

I'M... SORRY FOR WHAT I SAID BEFORE--ALL THOSE THINGS ABOUT YOUR FATHER AND SUCH.

BUT THIS, I'M AFRAID, IS GOOD-BYE.

BUT... BUT, I THOUGHT... WE CAN--

NO. WE CAN'T.

THERE'S TOO MUCH UGLINESS BETWEEN US, DIAN. AND EVEN IF IT'S NOT OF OUR OWN MAKING, IT'S ALSO BEYOND OUR CAPACITY FOR FIXING IT.

THE WORLD MUST CHANGE BEFORE WE CAN, I'M AFRAID.

WELL, MICKEY...

...WHAT DO YOU SAY TO A STIFF BELT BEFORE WE'RE KNEE-DEEP IN GOOKS ONCE AGAIN?

SOUNDS FINE, LIEUTENANT.

HOW ABOUT McSORLEY'S? THAT'S ON THE WAY DOWNTOWN.

22

SWELL. CHRIST, I WISH THIS WHOLE MESS WAS OV-- EH?

WHAT THE HELL'S *THIS?*

BET I KNOW WHO THAT SOMEBODY WAS...

HIS ARM'S HACKED UP PRETTY BAD. SOMEBODY BANDAGED IT, BUT WE BETTER GET HIM TO A HOSPITAL, PRONTO.

"LOOK BEYOND SKIN AND THERE YOU WILL FIND THE REALMS OF THE SOUL, BLEAK AND UNKIND. EVIL KNOWS NAUGHT BUT ITS OWN GREEDY AIMS. THE CHINATOWN MURDERS WERE OF THIS MAN'S REFRAIN."

SIGNED, "THE SANDMAN."

I'LL BE GOD DAMNED!!

YES, DADDY?

HELLO, DEAR.

I... WANTED TO SPEAK TO YOU ABOUT... EVERYTHING.

THERE'S BEEN A RESOLUTION TO THE SITUATION IN CHINATOWN.

OH?

YES. IT SEEMS THE ORIENTAL COMMUNITY WAS MORE OF A VICTIM THAN ANYONE.

SOMEONE WAS DELIBERATELY TRYING TO CAUSE A WAR BETWEEN THE TONG SOCIETIES.

I--I WANT TO APOLOGIZE...

WHO WAS BEHIND IT ALL, DADDY? WHO'S RESPONSIBLE FOR ALL THESE DEATHS?

23

STRANGELY ENOUGH, IT WAS HERMAN ROSS'S PARTNER, ELDRIDGE BENSON, THROUGH THE USE OF SOME HIRED KILLER.

SEEMS HE HAS A TRACE OF ASIAN BLOOD IN HIS LINEAGE AND THE ONLY PERSON WHO KNEW THIS FACT WAS ONE OF THE TONG LEADERS, A MAN NAMED WU SUNG.

BENSON HOPED THAT WU SUNG WOULD BE A CASUALTY OF ANY ALL-OUT WAR. APPARENTLY, BENSON'S COUNTRY CLUB IS EXCLUSIVE TO WHITES. HE BROKE DOWN AND CONFESSED ALL THIS AFTER BEING CAPTURED BY THE SANDMAN.

THE SANDMAN?!

AFTER ALL THE THINGS I HAD SAID: WELL, I-I FEEL A BIT FOOLISH NOW.

DON'T, DADDY. YOUR REASONS WERE WRONG, BUT JIMMY AND I HAVE DECIDED NOT TO SEE EACH OTHER AGAIN.

WHATEVER YOU DECIDE IS FINE. I LOVE YOU A BIT TOO MUCH SOME-TIMES.

GOOD NIGHT, DEAR.

GOOD NIGHT, DADDY.

RING RING

HELLO?

WESLEY! HELLO! NO, IT'S ALL RIGHT. I WAS STILL UP.

WHY, YES. AS A MATTER OF FACT I *AM* FREE FOR DINNER THIS WEEKEND.

T H E • E N D

-THE BRUTE-

"I can see
          nothing
     except
          the children:

struggling against
     the inevitable,

          trapped by
               a world
          gone mad
               with
               desires."

**FACE THE
DARK DREAMS
OF THE SANDMAN.**

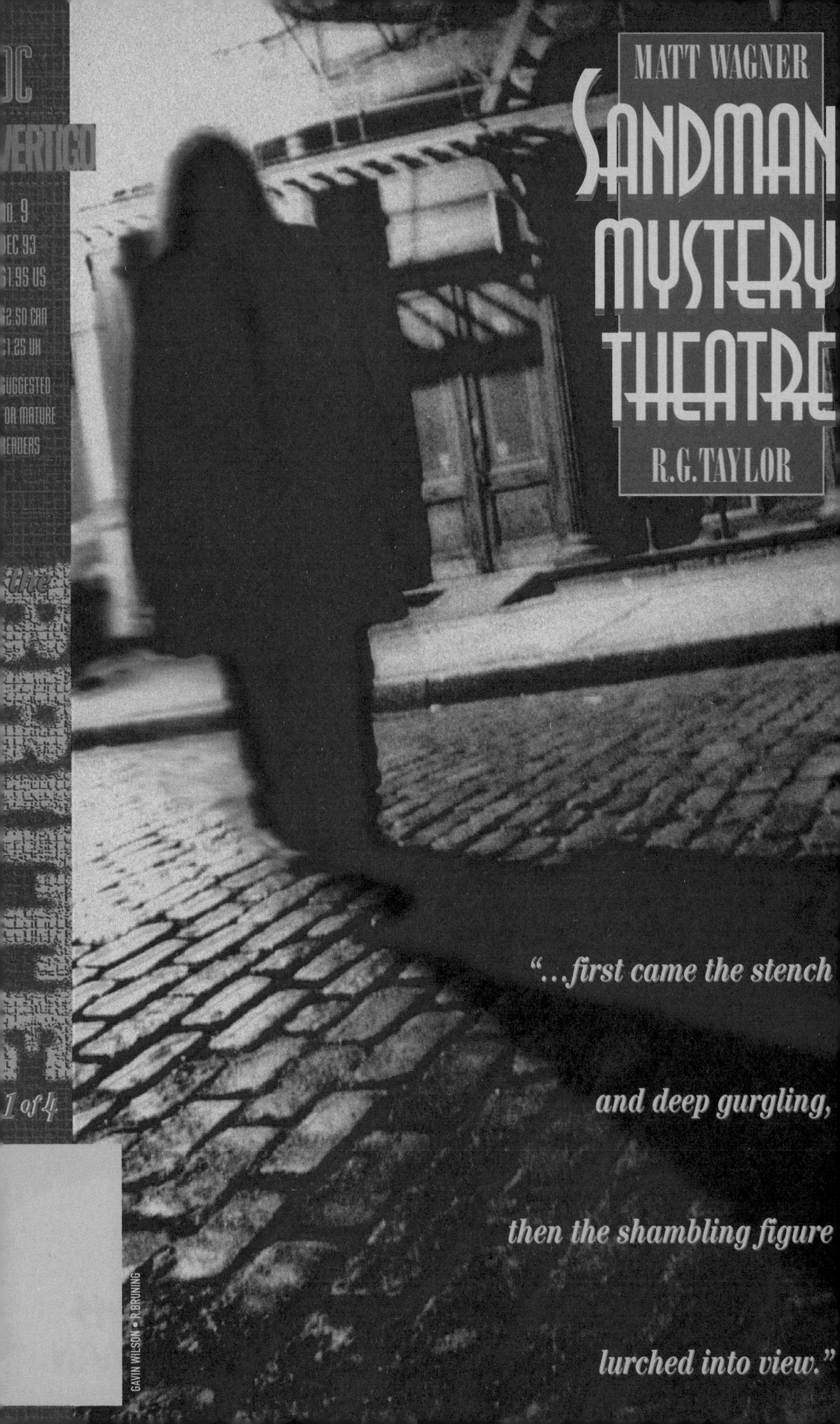

DC
VERTIGO
o. 9
EC 93
1.95 US
2.50 CAN
1.25 UK
UGGESTED
OR MATURE
EADERS
the
1 of 4
MATT WAGNER
SANDMAN
MYSTERY
THEATRE
R.G.TAYLOR
"...first came the stench
and deep gurgling,
then the shambling figure
lurched into view."
GAVIN WILSON • R.BRUNING

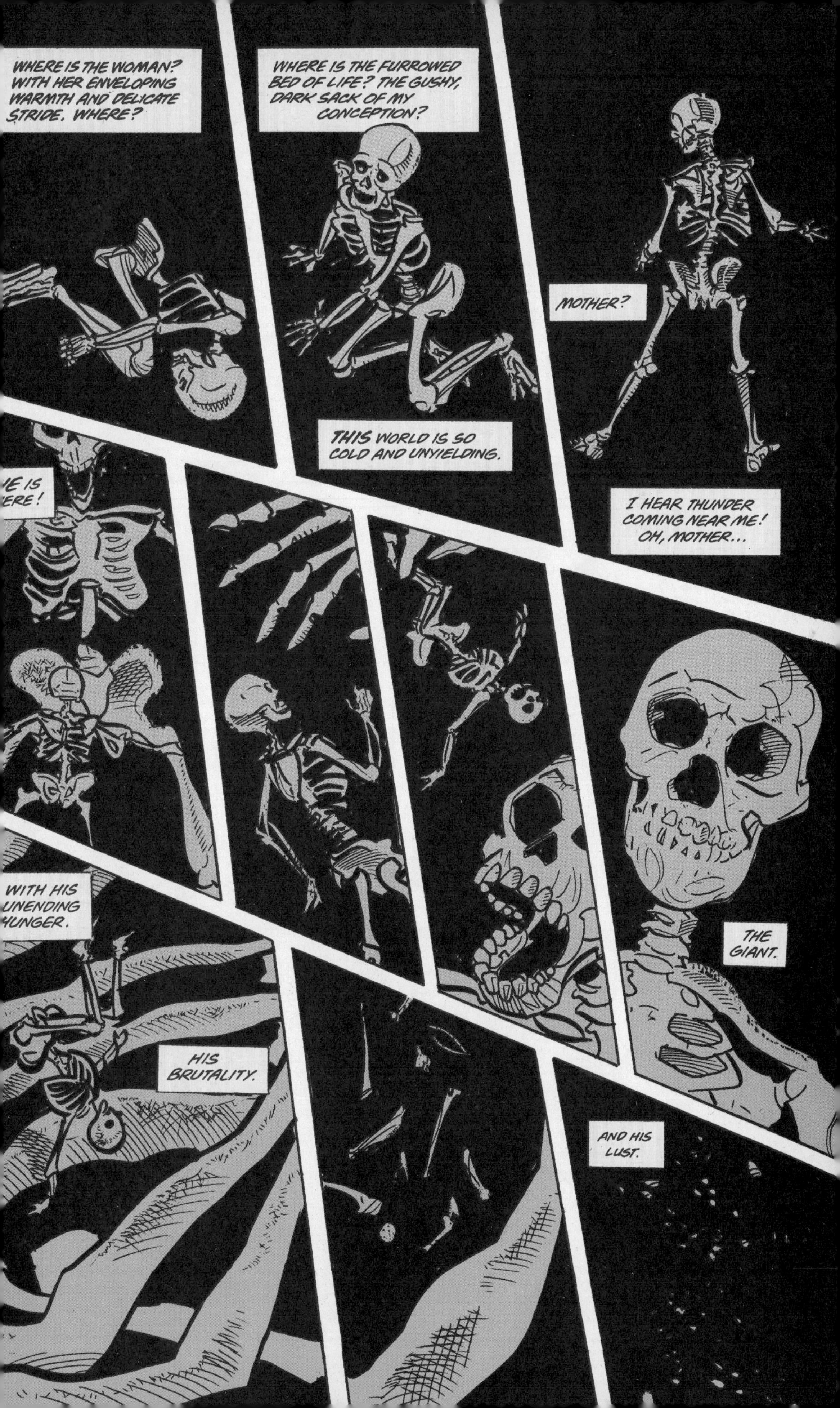

WHERE IS THE WOMAN? WITH HER ENVELOPING WARMTH AND DELICATE STRIDE. WHERE?
WHERE IS THE FURROWED BED OF LIFE? THE GUSHY, DARK SACK OF MY CONCEPTION?
THIS WORLD IS SO COLD AND UNYIELDING.
MOTHER?
I HEAR THUNDER COMING NEAR ME! OH, MOTHER...
THE GIANT.
WITH HIS UNENDING HUNGER.
HIS BRUTALITY.
AND HIS LUST.

THE DREAMS CONTINUE TO HAUNT ME. BUT AT LEAST MY WAKING HOURS ARE FULL... BOREDOM COULD KILL ME AT THIS POINT.

WELL, ISN'T THIS NICE?

I'M SO PLEASED YOU WERE FREE THIS EVENING, DIAN.

SO AM I.

I FEEL I'VE HAD MORE THAN MY SHARE OF NIGHT CLUBS AND SCANDALS FOR A WHILE. A LONG, LONG WHILE.

A QUIET DINNER IS JUST WHAT THE DOCTOR ORDERED.

I'M GLAD.

BUT, I HAD HEARD THE PROBLEMS IN CHINATOWN HAVE QUIETED DOWN QUITE A BIT.

MMM. ONCE THE REAL CULPRIT WAS DISCOVERED.

I MEAN..., THE TONGS ARE QUITE REAL, SO I DON'T IMAGINE THIS IS THE ABSOLUTE END OF TROUBLE IN THAT AREA.

CRIME KNOWS NEITHER RACE NOR CLASS.

AND... WHAT ABOUT YOUR FRIEND, JIMMY?

WELL ... IT'S LIKE YOU JUST SAID...

I -- I PROBABLY WON'T BE SEEING HIM AGAIN.

WAS THAT YOUR DECISION?

NO, BUT I CAN SEE THE SENSE IN IT.

JIMMY HAS STRONG FEELINGS ABOUT HIS PLACE IN THE WORLD.

AH...LOOK, CAN WE TALK ABOUT SOMETHING ELSE?

OF COURSE, I'M SORRY.

LISTEN, WHAT DO YOU WANT TO DO LATER? I WAS GOING TO SUGGEST THAT WE COULD GO TO HARLEM. I KNOW YOU LOVE THE JAZZ CLUBS.

MMM-MAYBE.

YOU SOUND LIKE YOU DON'T LIKE IT.

WHAT, JAZZ?

OH, I LIKE IT JUST FINE, BUT I'M NOT WILD ABOUT THESE WHITE SWING BANDS REALLY.

IT JUST SEEMS POPULAR MUSIC HAS BECOME A BACK-DROP TO HAVING A GOOD TIME-- AND LESS ABOUT EVERYDAY LIFE.

YES, YOU'RE RIGHT.

WHAT STARTED AS SOMETHING FRESH AND ORIGINAL IS NOW JUST ANOTHER WAY FOR SOME DANCEHALL PROMOTER TO FILL HIS POCKETS.

EXACTLY. BUT YOU KNOW I DO LIKE THIS STYLE COMING OUT OF THE SOUTH AND CHICAGO. THEY CALL IT RHYTHM AND BLUES. IT'S BASED ON JAZZ BUT IT'S EVEN CRUDER. VERY PASSIONATE AND TRUE.

FULL OF TEARS AND SEX.

OH! WELL, I... HAVEN'T REALLY HEARD IT.

STILL, I SAY LET'S EXTEND DINNER THROUGH-OUT THE EVENING.

THIS IS THE LONGEST OPPORTUNITY WE'VE HAD TO REALLY GET TO KNOW ONE ANOTHER. LET'S MAKE IT LAST.

SOUNDS GOOD TO ME.

CHEERS.

3

AND SO, WE DID JUST THAT. INTRIGUE AND DELIGHT FILLING OUR THOUGHTS. MURDER GRATEFULLY FORGOTTEN--FOR NOW.

A'SSS A LOVERLY SET YA GOT ON YA, LASS...

CHRIST! WHA'S Y'NAME AGIN...?

: snicker : TONI, Y'LIMEY... : hic : ...LIMEYS TALK SO GODDAMN CUTE.

WHA'S IT TAKE FOR A BIT O' THE PIE, THEN-- EH?

J--JUS' A QUICK TASTE. AH BUY YA' A BOTT'L O' RUM...

OW' 'BOUT IT, TONI-LOVE?

RUM'S FOR LITTLE GIRLS, POPEYE.

DO YER BEST AN THEN YOU C'N BUY ME SOME SCOTCH.

UNNHHH...

YOU DIRTY THING.

COR! WHAT A SET! MMMM-NNHMM...

: SMACK :

YOU BIG HARD DIRTY THING...

GASP!

GASP!

GASP!

THE BRUTE
A C T · O N E

NNN--
AAAAGGH!

AT
A...?

BULLOCKS!
OULD YA *HOLD STILL!*
IN'T E'EN GOT 'ER
IN YET...

NNAAA! NNAAA!
LOOK, YOU STOOPID
BASTARD!! LOOOOK...!

UNH...?

⑤

GLLCK--

KRRACK!

WH-UMPH...!

KLUD!

WHU...
WHUZZA PR-

THN

UNNGHH...

FUD

PRAK

KRRACK

D...

KRRACK

D-D...

KRUNCH

DON'...

SKLUUTCH

...DON'!...HURTMETOO... DON'HURT... GOOGIRL... TREET-CHU-RIGH... GOOGIRL...

WELL, HERE WE ARE. AND I THINK DADDY IS WORKING LATE TONIGHT.

UM... CARE TO COME IN FOR A DRINK?

WELLLL... GOT ANY LEMONADE?

HA!

OH, WES, I'M SORRY, EVEN AFTER AN EVENING OUT WITH YOU, I FORGET. IT'S JUST THAT... WELL, EVERYBODY DRINKS.

ALMOST EVERYONE.

NO, I HAVE A BUSY SCHEDULE TOMORROW, SO I THINK I'LL JUST SAY GOOD NIGHT.

AND THANK YOU.

AND I THINK I JUST MIGHT FAINT, GALLANT SIR.

MMM... BUT YOUR PERFUME'S MAKING ME FEEL OTHERWISE. I'D BETTER GO.

GOOD NIGHT, DIAN. I'LL CALL YOU AGAIN, SOON.

GOOD NIGHT, WES. AND THANKS AGAIN FOR A MARVELOUS TIME.

I AM NOT USED TO MY EVENINGS BEING SO PLEASANT.

⑦

NOR TO RISING SO EARLY IN THE MORNING. UP BEFORE NOON...

I AM UTTERLY UNLIKE DEAR THOMAS IN THIS REGARD. THE PROVERBIAL EARLY BIRD, I HAD ASKED HIM TO JOIN ME FOR LUNCH WITH A POTENTIAL NEW BUSINESS COLLEAGUE.

THANKS AGAIN FOR COMING TODAY, THOMAS.

CERTAINLY, M'BOY.

YOU SAID YOU'RE MEETING ARTHUR REISLING, DIDN'T YOU? AS IN, ARTHUR REISLING, THE FIGHT PROMOTER?

THE SAME.

BUT THAT'S JUST ONE OF HIS MANY ENTERPRISES.

YES, I KNOW. THEY SAY THE OLD FELLOW'S GOT MORE MONEY THAN HE KNOWS WHAT TO DO WITH.

YES, WELL, HE'S APPROACHED ME ABOUT CO-FINANCING A SCIENTIFIC EXPEDITION TO ANTARCTICA. I'M CURIOUS TO SEE WHAT YOUR IMPRESSIONS OF HIM ARE AS WELL.

WHAT KIND OF MAN MIXES BOXING AND PHILANTHROPY?

A FULL-BLOODED ONE, SIR. MR. DODDS?

WH--?

OH, YES. AND YOU MUST BE ARTHUR REISLING?

THAT I AM, MR. DODDS. THAT I AM.

AND DON'T FEEL BAD IF MY PRESENCE... CONFUSES YOU. I'M QUITE USED TO SUCH REACTIONS.

UHH... YES. MAY I INTRODUCE JUDGE THOMAS SCHAEFFER?

AH. A MAN OF THE BENCH! WONDERFUL.

RETIRED. AND, YES, WESLEY WAS JUST EXPLAINING YOUR INTEREST IN ANTARCTICA.

8

INDEED. MARVELOUS PLACE.

IT IS AN UNTAPPED WELLSPRING OF NATURAL RESOURCES. THE WORLD WILL LEARN SUCH LESSONS ONLY AT THE COST OF OUR OWN INVESTMENTS.

MAYBE SO.

I HAVE HEARD THAT YOU MADE A GREAT DEAL OF YOUR FORTUNE ABROAD, MR. REISLING.

YOU ARE EXPERIENCED AT THIS.

ARTHUR, PLEASE.

YES, I SPENT MUCH OF MY YOUTH DELVING INTO THE MARKETS OF CHILE AND SOUTH AFRICA.

DESOLATE CORNERS THAT THE WORLD ALL BUT FORGETS.

RIPE FOR THE PICKING, I'VE FOUND.

AND NOW YOU'VE SET YOUR SIGHTS FURTHER SOUTH.

THE FURTHEST.

THE MEEK ONLY DIE YOUNG, GENTLEMEN. YES, WE SHOULD DISCUSS THIS MORE FULLY AT MY OFFICES. BUT FOR NOW... MAY I OFFER YOU TWO TICKETS TO THIS EVENING'S FIGHTS. NO TITLE BOUTS, I'M AFRAID.

I DON'T--

EH, THAT IS... I'M AFRAID MY EVENING IS ALREADY FILLED, ARTHUR. THANKS, ANYWA--

BUT *I* WOULD CERTAINLY LOVE TO GO.

IF YOU CAN EASILY SPARE THESE, THAT IS.

THEY'RE YOURS.

WELL, LET'S SCHEDULE A PRESENTATION MEETING, DODDS. SHALL WE SAY SOME TIME NEXT WEEK, THEN?

YES, THAT WOULD BE FINE.

PREFERABLY IN THE AFTERNOON.

SPLENDID.

OH, AND BY THE WAY, WHY DON'T YOU COME TO A ST. PATRICK'S DAY PARTY AT MY HOUSE THIS SATURDAY? ONE O'CLOCK. CALL ME IF YOU NEED A DATE ARRANGED.

NO, THAT'S FINE. I'LL SEE YOU THERE.

EXCELLENT.

9

AND NOW, ROUND TWO OF "IRON DOG" STINSON VS. "ROCKET" EDDIE RAMSEY!

BOOOO

YAAAAHH!

RAMSEY, YA BUM!!

GODDAMN FAIRIES!!

HSSSSS--

THAK!

BLEEDIN' ASSHOLE!!

TWO-BIT MICK SONUVABI--

GET UP!!

ONE!

BOOOO!

WEASEL SHIT!

BLACK-EYED PANSY!

STAY DOWN!

BLUBBER GUT!

TWO! THREE! FOUR! FIVE! SIX!

GET UP, RAMSEY!

GET UP!

SEVEN! EIGHT!

NINE!

GLAD YOU COULD JOIN ME TONIGHT, BELMONT.

THANKS FOR ASKING, JUDGE. I JUST HOPE THE NEXT BOUT'S MORE EXCITING THAN THIS ONE.

YES. NOT MUCH FUEL IN HIS ROCKET, IS THERE?

TEN!!

DING-DING! DING-DING!

⑩

RAMSEY, YOU STUPID GODDAMN ASSHOLE!!

SORRY, MEL...

SORRY?! SORRY FOR STANDIN' IN FRONT OF THAT SCUMBAG'S PUNCHES?!

YOU SEEM TO FORGET THAT I GOT A STAKE IN THIS TOO.!!

IF YOU DON'T TAKE NO PURSE, THEN I DON'T GET NO TRAINER'S CUT!

I KNOW, MEL. I'M REAL SORRY. NEXT TIME, I SWE--

"NEXT TIME"?!

AHH...YOU MAKE ME SICK! WHO SAYS THERE'S GONNA BE A NEXT TIME? OR THAT IT'LL BE ANY DIFFERENT!

TOUGH BREAK OUT THERE, PAL.

YOU GOT KNOCKED AROUND HARD. AND YOU WERE MOVIN' PRETTY SLOW. WHEN WAS THE LAST TIME THAT YOU ATE ANYTHING? I MEAN THAT HAD MEAT IN IT.

WHAT'S IT TO YA, MISTER?

I'M INTERESTED IN YOUR WELFARE.

NOW, WHY WOULD A FIGHTER NOT BE EATIN' WELL BEFORE A MATCH? COULD BE, HE'S GOT OTHER--MORE IMPORTANT--EXPENSES.

I'M HERE TO MAKE YOU AN OFFER, PAL. IF YOU EVER CARE TO MAKE SOME GUARANTEED DOUGH ON A FIGHT--GIVE ME A CALL. I RUN A FEW "UNOFFICIAL" BOUTS ON THE SIDE.

BLACK-MARKET BRAWLS? I COULD BE BARRED FROM REAL FIGHTS FOR THAT.

DEPENDS ON YOUR NEEDS, I GUESS.

I KNOW YOU'D EARN THE MONEY.

THE DREAMS HAVE ALWAYS LED ME TO PLACES I HAD NEVER BEEN. TO MYSTERIES I MIGHT NEVER'VE EXPLORED.

THE SANDS OF TIME DRIFT OVER MY LIFE AND MY DESIRES.

BURYING ME IN A DARK UNDERWORLD OF CORRUPTION.

A WORLD I WOULDN'T HAVE KNOWN OTHERWISE.

CLICK

DIAN?

DIAN, I'M HOME!

ARE YOU STILL UP?!

I'M IN HERE, DADDY!

12

WHAT IS IT THAT SUCKS AT MY SOUL SO ACUTELY?

WHAT EMPTINESS DRIVES ME OUT INTO THE NIGHT TIME AND AGAIN?

TO FIGHT FORCES I CANNOT HOPE TO DEFEAT.

EMILY? I'M... I'M HOME!

OH, DADDY! I'M SO GLAD YOU'RE HOME!

YOU SHOULD HAVE SEEN WHAT HAPPENED DOWN IN THE ALLEY EARLIER! MRS. PETRILLO WAS HITTING HER HUSBAND WITH AN IRON!

I THOUGHT I TOLD YOU TO IGNORE ALL THAT NONSENSE!!

I'M...I'M SORRY, HONEY. I KNOW YOU GET LONELY HERE.

I JUST-- JUST FEEL SO BAD ABOUT HAVING TO LEAVE YOU ALONE LIKE THIS SO MUCH.

IT'S OKAY, DADDY.

I KNOW YOU'RE WORKING HARD FOR US, AND SOMEDAY WE'LL BUY A HOUSE, AND I'LL BE ALLOWED BACK IN SCHOOL, AND...

OHHH...YOUR FACE...

YOU...LOST AGAIN, DIDN'T YOU?

WHO ME? NAHHH... I JUST TOOK SECOND PLACE!

13

OHH, DADDY...

;KOFF!... A--HACK! HACK! HACK! KOFF!... HACK! HACK! HACK! HACK!... A-HACK! HACK! KOFF! KOFF!

...KOFF! ...KOFF!

HOW MUCH MEDICINE IS THERE LEFT, BABY?

NOT... ;KOFF KOFF;... NOT MUCH. I'VE BEEN TRYING TO SAVE IT FOR WHEN I REALLY NEED IT...

KLACK-A-TA-KLACK-A-TA-KLACK-A-TA-KLACK--

--ACK-A-

HANG ON, SWEETHEART.

--KLACK-A-

I'M ;KOFF!;... ...I'M USED TO IT, DADDY.

I-I'VE GOT TO RUN OUT NOW FOR JUST A BIT, BABY.

I NEED TO CALL SOMEONE ABOUT SOME SPARE WORK I WAS OFFERED. BUT I'LL BE RIGHT BACK. I PROMISE.

KLACK-A-T.

IT'S OKAY, DADDY.

I KNOW NOT TO OPEN THE DOOR FOR ANY STRANGERS.

AND REMEMBER DADDY, NO MATTER WHAT HAPPENS...

..."ROCKET" RAMSEY WILL ALWAYS BE MY CHAMPION!

WHAM! POW! OH, SWEETHEART, YOU SHOULD HAVE **SEEN** IT!

SO, YOU HAD A GOOD TIME THEN?

KRAK! BAM! MOST OF THE FIGHTS WERE FAIRLY DULL. BUT THERE WAS THIS ONE LIGHT HEAVYWEIGHT...

...NAME OF BILLY CONN.

HONEY, YOU SHOULD HAVE **SEEN** THIS FELLOW CONNECT!!

WHAM! POW!

BOXING IS MAN STUFF, DADDY. I'LL JUST TAKE YOUR WORD FOR--

NOW, WAIT! LET ME JUST TELL YOU ABOUT ROUND SEVEN. FIRST, HE--

RING-RING RING-RING

OH, DAMN IT ALL! HOLD THAT THOUGHT, DIAN...

SAVED BY DE BELL... HOO BOY!

RING

BELMONT HOUSEHOLD.

YES. THIS IS HE.

WHY...YESSS, I REMEMBER YOU. WHAT DO YOU WANT?

MEET WITH ME? WHAT ON EARTH FOR?

ON **WHO?**

THE ARTHUR REISLING?! VERY WELL THEN, TOMORROW NIGHT. WHERE AND WHEN?

⑮

THANKS AGAIN FOR INVITING ME ALONG, WES-- *YOW!* SOME DIGS!

YES, MR. REISLING DOESN'T SEEM TO BE SUBTLE ABOUT MUCH OF ANYTHING. AND THANKS FOR COMING.

BUT I'M AFRAID I DO HAVE A SMALL CONFESSION TO MAKE. IT'S NOT ONLY THAT I LOOKED FORWARD TO SPENDING MORE TIME WITH YOU...

OHHHH...?

WELL, I WAS... EAVESDROPPING ON DADDY AGAIN THE OTHER NIGHT AND I OVERHEARD HIM GET A TIP THAT SOUNDED LIKE IT WAS DIRT ON ARTHUR REISLING. SO WHEN YOU CALLED TO INVITE ME TO A PARTY AT THIS SAME PERSON'S HOUSE... *UHHH,* NOT THAT I WOULDN'T HAVE GONE WITH YOU ANYWAY, THAT IS...

I... FIND MYSELF TAKING A PERVERSE PLEASURE IN SPYING ON DADDY'S CASES LIKE THIS.

THE CRIMINAL WORLD IS... INTRIGUING. WELL, WE'LL JUST HAVE TO KEEP OUR EARS OPEN THEN, WON'T WE?

YOUR HAT, SIR?

NO, THANKS.

AHHH, DODDS! WONDERFUL! GLAD YOU COULD MAKE IT, OLD BOY. MOST EXCELLENT.

YOU'RE ACTUALLY LUCKY TO HAVE CAUGHT ME LIKE THIS. I WAS JUST ON MY WAY TO TAKE A PHONE CALL IN MY DEN. THE PARTY'S AROUND BACK--

SISSY BRAT!

CANDY PANTS!!

16

...IN THE GARDEN. BOYS! HELP YOURSELVES TO A DRIN-- *I SAID,* *"BOYS!"*

SNOT FACE!! I BEAT YOU!

DID NOT, STINKY BUTT!

DID TOO!

DID NOT!

DID TOO!

STAND UP NOW!

LOOK SHARP!

MR. DODDS, THESE ARE MY YOUNGEST BOYS-- CHARLES AND TOBIAS.

BOYS... SAY HELLO TO MR. DODDS AND...

I'M AFRAID I DON'T KNOW YOUR LOVELY FRIEND'S NAME.

HELLO!

AND GOODBYE! (giggle)

DIAN BELMONT, MR. REISLING. THOSE TWO LOOK LIKE QUITE A HANDFUL!

MMM? YES, I SUPPOSE...

THANK YOU, ARTHUR.

WELL, AS I SAID, I'M OFF TO TAKE A CALL. FEEL FREE TO LOOK AROUND AND HELP YOURSELVES TO A DRINK FROM THE BAR. SEE YOU IN THE GARDEN...

MY, MY, MY...

AND THAT'S COMING FROM YOU! YEESH!

17

SO HOW DO YOU KNOW THIS FELLOW? OBVIOUSLY, YOU DON'T KNOW HIM WELL.

NO, THAT'S TRUE.

NOTHING PAST HIS PUBLIC NOTORIETY.

HE WANTS ME TO CO-SPONSOR INDUSTRIAL DEVELOPMENTS IN ANTARCTICA WITH HIM. I HAVEN'T YET DECIDED WHETHER THAT'S A GOOD IDEA OR NOT.

I'VE HAD DR-- CALL IT A FEELING THAT HE'S NOT TO BE TRUSTED.

AND NOW THERE'S THIS STUFF WITH YOUR FATHER--

OH. SORRY THERE, BROTHER.

UNP--!

JUST STOPPED IN FOR A REFILL.

I'M DENNIS REISLING. SORRY, DIDN'T CATCH THE NAME. MR...?

DODDS. WESLEY DODDS.

OH.

YES. YOU'RE FATHER'S NEW "FRIEND."

WELL...

I WILL SAY YOU DON'T LOOK LIKE MOST OF ARTHUR'S FRIENDS.

FOR ONE THING YOU'RE NOT A BLOND.

AND YOU SEEM ALTOGETHER SOBER-- UNLIKE THE REST OF US! SEE IF YOU CAN'T REMEDY THAT, BROTHER.

SO...

I'M BACK TO THE PARTY. I'M SURE FATHER WILL JOIN YOU SOON.

I'M SURE.

WELL, WELL... LOOKS LIKE YOU DON'T MEET THE LOCAL CRITERIA.

NOT NEARLY BLOND ENOUGH!

NOT NEARLY DULL ENOUGH!

HO HUM.

124

THERE HE IS, ROSS.

WANT ME TO COME WITH YOU, LARRY?

NO. HE SAID HE WANTED TO SPEAK TO ME ALONE.

BUT KEEP AN EYE ON HIM.

YOU GOT IT.

THANKS FOR COMIN'!

IT IS REALLY YOU. YOU'RE LUCKY I REMEMBERED YOU FROM THAT FIGHT. IT WAS OVER RATHER QUICKLY.

YEAH, WELL...

LOOK, HERE'S WHAT I GOTTA SAY. THE OTHER NIGHT, AFTER THE FIGHT YOU SAW ME IN, ARTHUR REISLING OFFERED TO PAY ME TO FIGHT IN AN ILLEGAL MATCH.

REISLING, HIMSELF? WHY YOU? AND WHY ARE YOU TELLING ME THIS?

REISLING MUST FIGURE ME TOO LOW ON THE TOTEM POLE TO GIVE HIM ANY TROUBLE. BUT I'M BUILT BIG. I CAN TAKE A LOT OF PUNISHMENT IF I'M IN SHAPE. SPECTATORS LIKE THAT.

AND AS TO WHY I'M SQUEALIN'...

YEAH?

THAT SORTA SHIT COULD GET ME BARRED FROM FIGHTIN' FOR REAL. I COULDN'T DO THAT TO MY...TO MY FAMILY.

SO THIS IS IT FOR ME. KEEP YOUR EYE ON REISLING. TRAP HIM. SHOOT HIM. I DON'T CARE. JUST LEAVE ME THE HELL OUT OF IT.

YOU'RE OUT. AND THANKS.

⑲

UNHH...

UNHH...!
SOMEBODY?! SOMEBODY, HELP ME?! PLEASE?!

HEY, KID. WHAT'S WRONG?

I WAS RUNNIN' AN' TWISTED MY ANKLE. I THINK IT'S BROKE!

EASY, KID. HOLD ST-- UNK!

CHCKK

ALL RIGHT, YOU GUYS. GRAB 'IM!

HERE'S YER QUARTER, KID...
NOW, SCRAM!

CAN'T I STAY AND WATCH?!

I SAID, "SCRAM"! OR YOU'LL GET THE SAME!

OKAY, MISTER, OKAY!

HE'S ROUSIN', BOSS.

NUHHHNN...

20

THAT'S FAR ENOUGH.

WHU... WHAT IZZIT? WHAT DO YOU GUYS WANT?

SHUT UP, ASSHOLE.

HEY, LISTEN, YOU GUYS. I DON'T KNOW WHAT YOU'RE ALL TALK--

YEAH, BUDDY... YOU DONE SAID WAY TOO MUCH AS IT IS. AND TO ALL THE WRONG PEOPLE AS WELL.

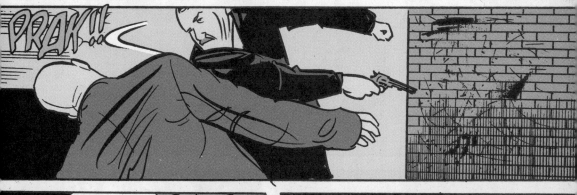

PRAK!!

THERE YOU GO TALKIN' AGAIN.

WHAT IS IT WITH THAT GODDAMN TONGUE O' YOURS? YOU THINK MR. REISLING MAKES OFFERS LIKE THAT TO MEATBALL GOONS LIKE YOU WITHOUT COVERIN' HIS TAIL?

THAT TONGUE OF YOURS... IT'S A STUPID TONGUE.

MAYBE YOU JUST SHOULDN'T EVEN HAVE SUCH A STUPID TONGUE...

KLONK!

YAAAGGH~!

WHAT THE F-- LOOK OUT!

THERE HE GOES!!

SHIT, WHERE'D HE GO! WHERE IS HE?!

SHOOT 'IM! JUST SHOOT 'IM!

QUIET YOU ASS-HOLES!! LISTEN!!

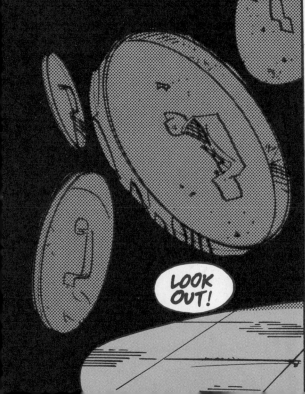

LOOK OUT!

YAAGH!!

KANG

BASTARD

K-KANG

22

EVER'BODY HOLD STILL! I GOT 'IM!

FOOSH!

AAACKK-- *JEEZUS* (choke) CHRISSSS...

BOSS! I GOT 'IM, BOSS, GET UP! DON'T MOVE, YOU SONUVABITCH!

DROP YOUR WEAPON OR FACE THE DARK REALMS OF YOUR DREAMING.

HERE, REUBEN! GET AWAY FROM HIM! I GOT A BETTER WAY TO HANDLE THIS...

TWEEEEE-

COME AND GET 'EM, BABY.

HEH.

㉓

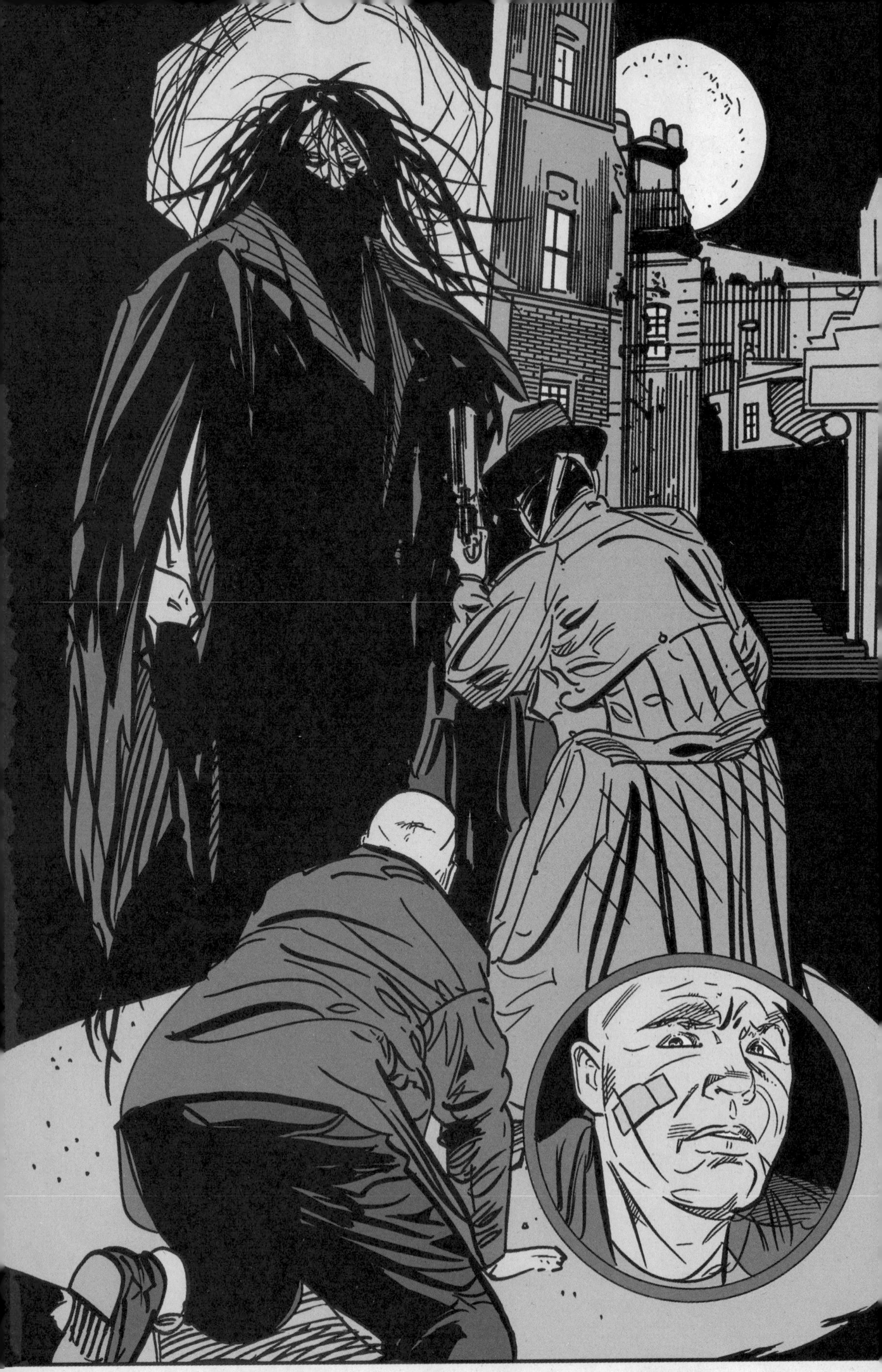

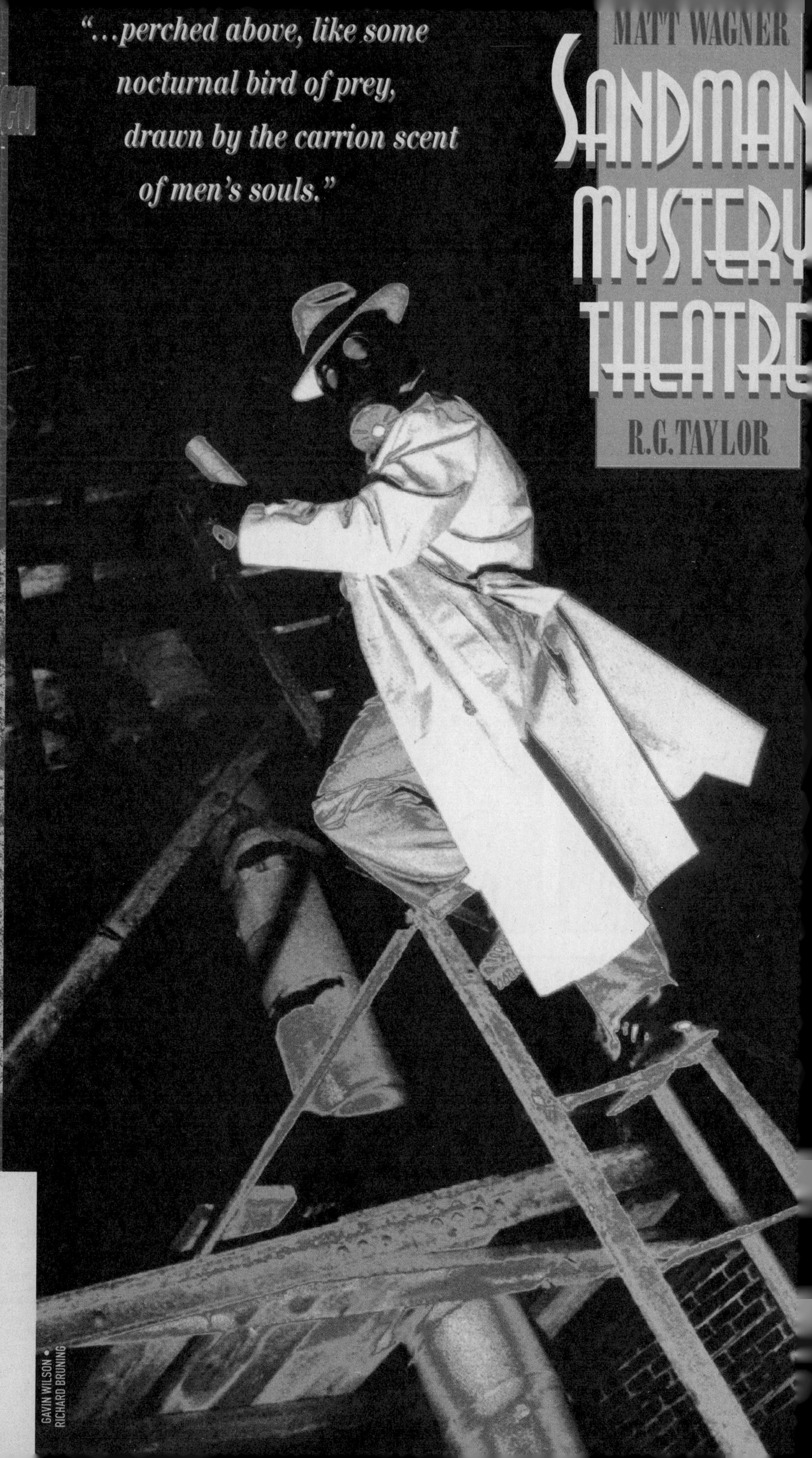

"...perched above, like some
nocturnal bird of prey,
drawn by the carrion scent
of men's souls."

MATT WAGNER

SANDMAN
MYSTERY
THEATRE

R.G. TAYLOR

GAVIN WILSON •
RICHARD BRUINING

Katharine **HEPBURN** Cary **GRANT**

BRINGING UP BABY with Charlie **RUGGLES**

WELL, THAT WAS FUN-- EH, DIAN? GOD SAVE ME FROM EVER HAVING KIDS-- BUT *NOT* FROM CARY GRANT! MY LORD, THAT MAN IS LUSCIOUS.

A TAD TOO PERFECT FOR MY TASTES.

WAIT TILL D'CROWD DIES DOWN, PAULEY.

MMM -- NOT FOR MINE. I HEAR RUMORS THAT HE'S ACTUALLY A FAERIE THOUGH.

LOOK, DERE'S MORE PICTURES AT THE ENTRANCE!

(Sigh) I SURE WOULD LOVE A SHOT AT CURING HIM OF THAT AFFLICTION!

IT'S NOT A DISEASE, CAROL.

I TINK DEY GOT STUFF FROM FLASH GORDON'S TRIP TO MARS !!

PAULEY...

I KNEW I'D FIND YOOS DOWN HERE AT DIS SIN-PALACE!

I TOLD YOOS T'STAY AWAY FROM HERE!!

AWW, MAAA! I JUST WANTED...

WHO GIVES A SHIT *WHAT* YOU WANT!

LISTEN TO WHAT I TELL YOU!!

OWW! MA, I--

AGH--

SHUT UP, LIL' BASTARD!!

DON'T GIVE ME NONE O' YER LIP!

I CARRIED YOU IN MY BODY FER NINE MONTHS...

AN' I **WON'T** TAKE NONE O' YER SMART-ASS MOUTH!

KRAK!

I'M SORRY, MA! I--

AGHH!!

THAT'S ENOUGH! STOP-- STOP HITTING HIM.

GODDAMN LITTLE--

EH?!

TAKE YER HANDS OFFA ME!!

HIGH-SOCIETY PRIG!!

I DON'T THINK THIS WILL HELP AT ALL.

HE KNOWS YOU'RE ANGRY.

IT'S THE ONLY WAY HE'LL LEARN-- LIKE *YOU* SHOULD'A LEARNED...

...TO MIND YER OWN BUSINESS!!

OH!! HOW DARE YOU...?

HERE *NOW!* WHAT'S ALL THIS ABOUT?

OHHH, NOTHING, YE GODDAMN FLATFOOT.

PEOPLE SHOULD JUST LEARN IS ALL.

LEARN TO STAY OUTTA UDDER PEOPLE'S FAMILY LIFE!!

②

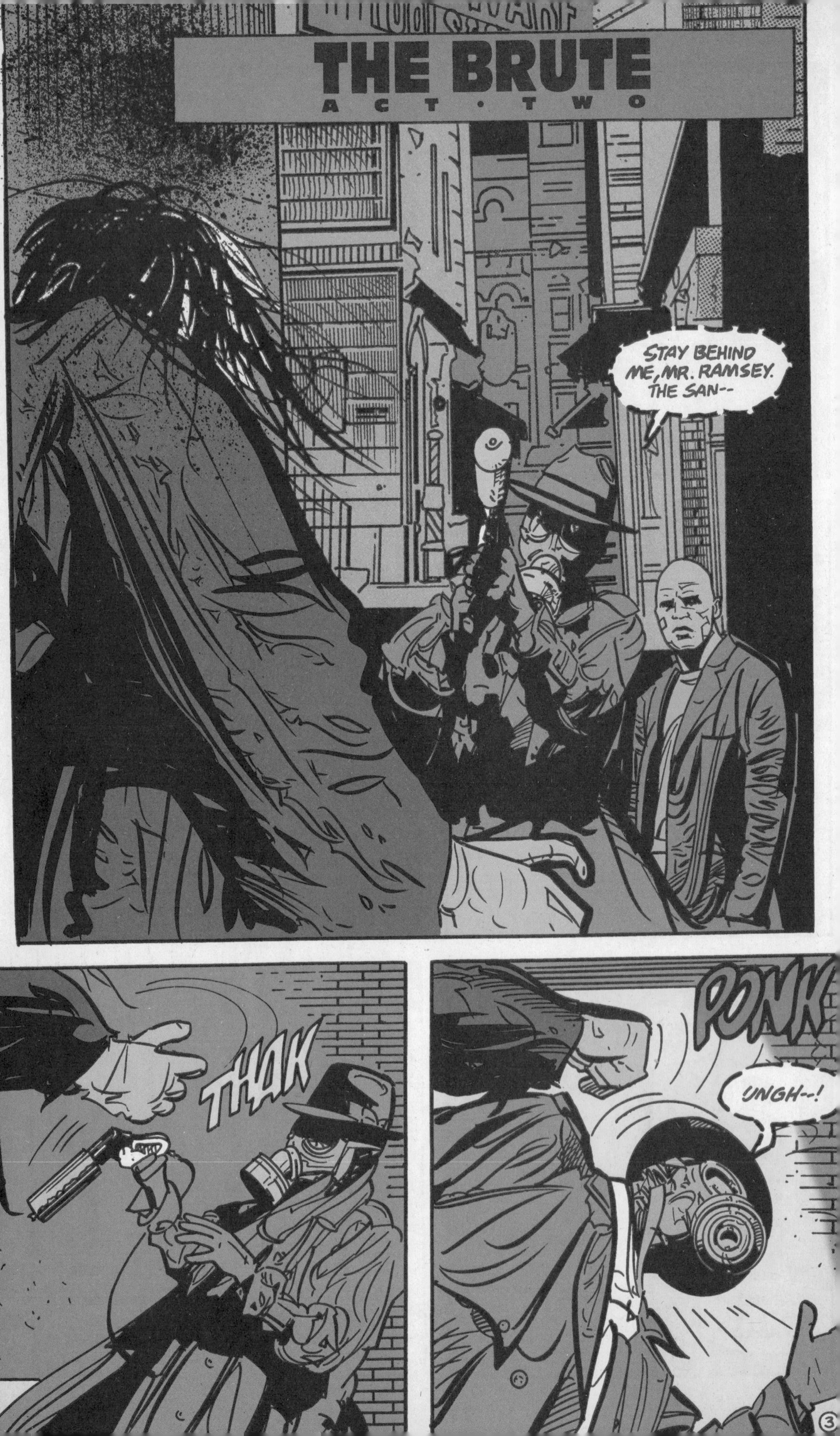

THE BRUTE
ACT • TWO
STAY BEHIND ME, MR. RAMSEY. THE SAN--
THAK
PONK
UNGH--!

ALL RIGHT, Y'BIG GORILLA!

YOU 'N ME!

NNMPH!

RRMPHTSS, DOONMPH...

C'MON!

THNK!

UNHH! THICK AS A BRICK!

BUT SLOW AS MOLASSES!

GOTCHU! HEY, BOSS, I GOT--

YYAAAA-UNK!

POW!

UUUNGH--

J-JEZUSSS...

4

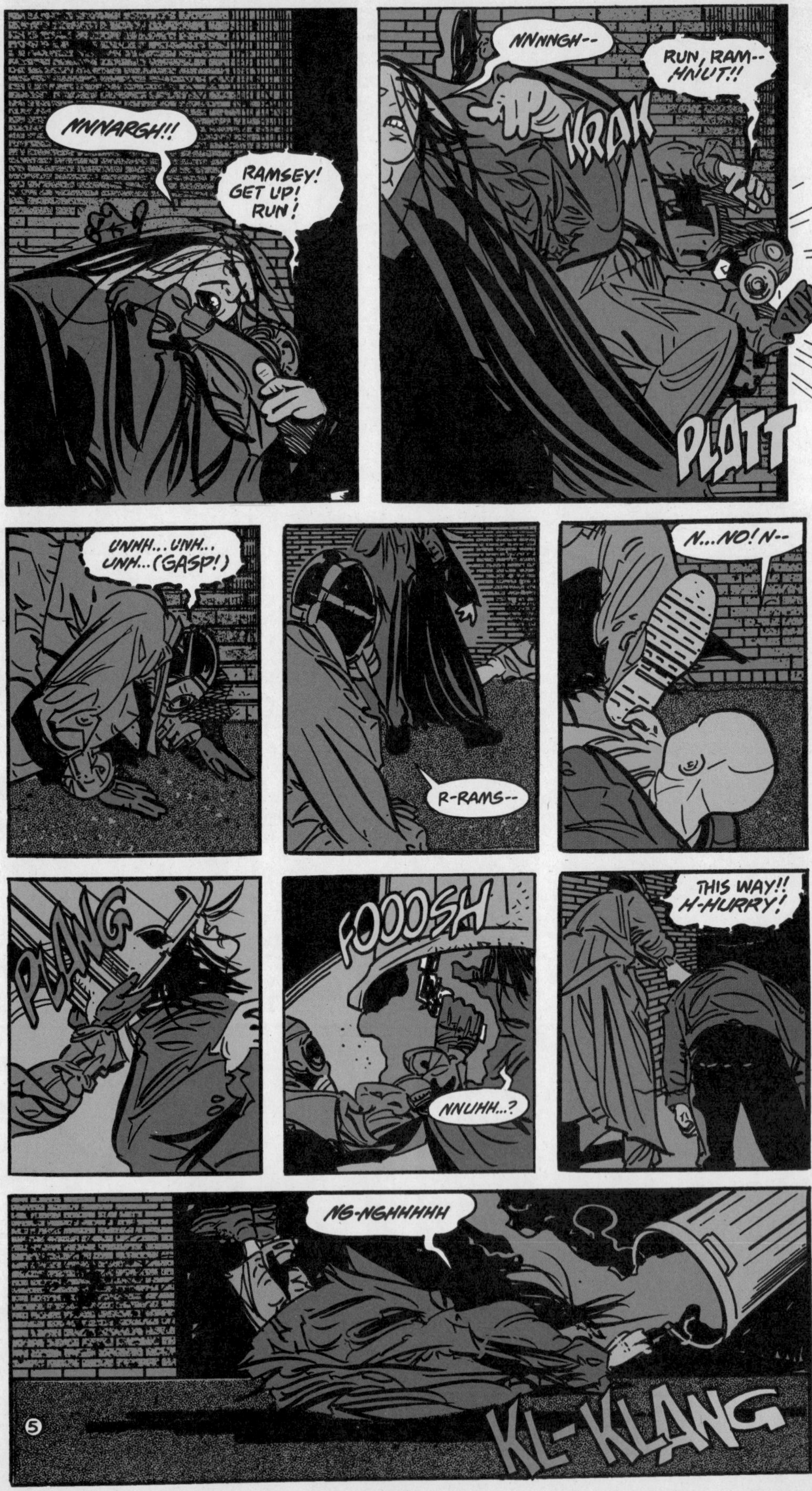
NNNARGH!!
RAMSEY! GET UP! RUN!
NNNNGH--
RUN, RAM--HNUT!!
KRAK
PLATT
UNNH... UNH... UNH...(GASP!)
R-RAMS--
N...NO! N--
PLANG
FOOOSH
NNUHH...?
THIS WAY!! H-HURRY!
NG-NGHHHHH
KL-KLANG

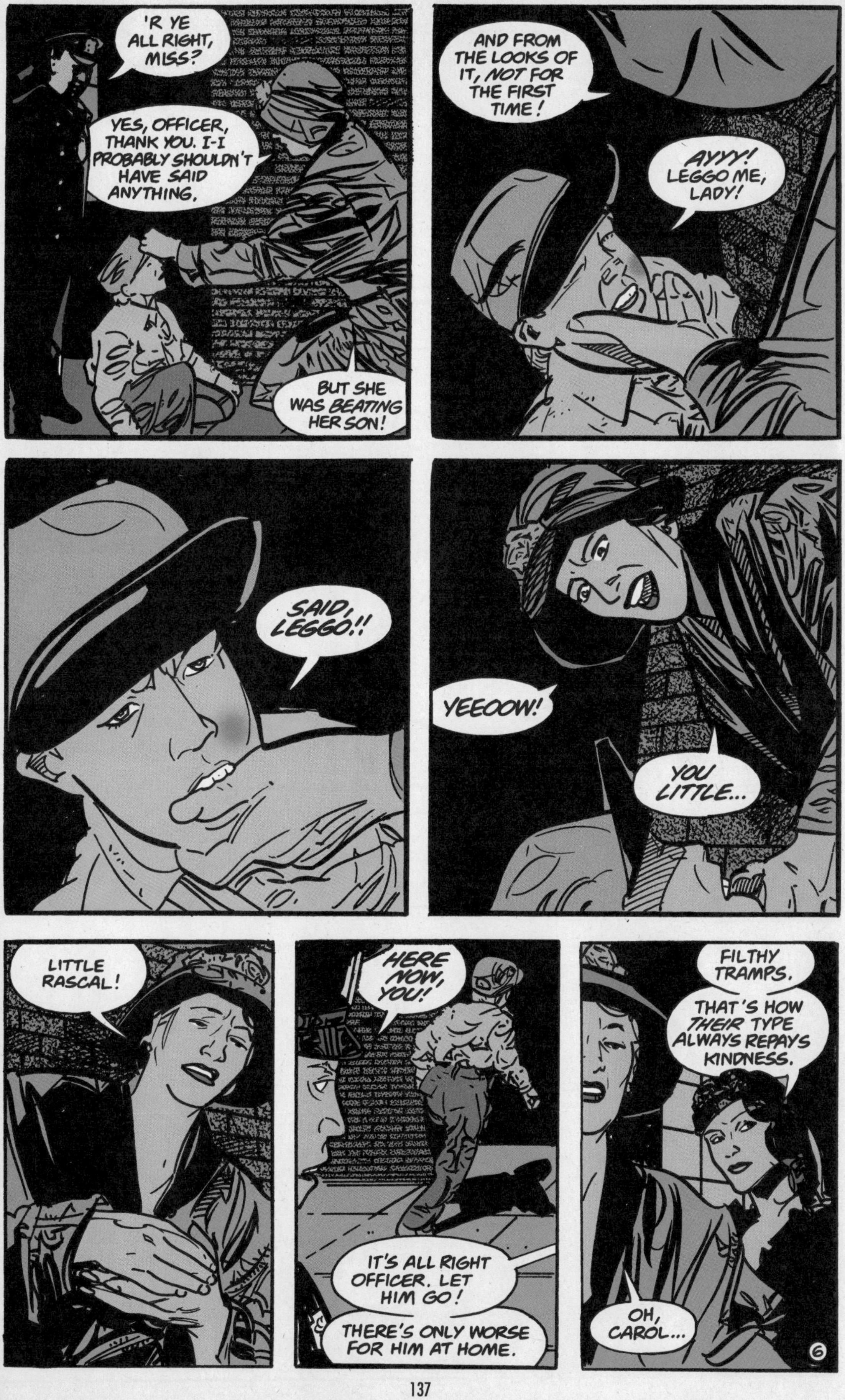
'R YE ALL RIGHT, MISS?
YES, OFFICER, THANK YOU. I-I PROBABLY SHOULDN'T HAVE SAID ANYTHING.
BUT SHE WAS BEATING HER SON!
AND FROM THE LOOKS OF IT, NOT FOR THE FIRST TIME!
AYYY! LEGGO ME, LADY!
SAID, LEGGO!!
YEEOOW!
YOU LITTLE...
LITTLE RASCAL!
HERE NOW, YOU!
IT'S ALL RIGHT OFFICER. LET HIM GO!
THERE'S ONLY WORSE FOR HIM AT HOME.
FILTHY TRAMPS.
THAT'S HOW THEIR TYPE ALWAYS REPAYS KINDNESS.
OH, CAROL...
6

YOU ALL RIGHT, MISTER? YOU TOOK QUITE A CRACK TO THE RIBS BACK THERE.

I AM... I'LL BE FINE.

BUT I REC--RECOMMEND THAT YOU LOCATE A NEW RESIDENCE AT ONCE. REISLING'S MEN OBVIOUSLY KNOW WHERE YOU LIVE.

WHO THE HELL ARE YOU?

I AM... A FRIEND.

BUT GO NOW. HURRY.

"THE SANDS OF TIME RUN SWIFT."

EMILY!! ARE YOU-- ARE YOU ALL RIGHT?!

MMM?

I'M FINE, DADDY. WHAT'S WRONG?

NO -- NOTHING...

NO. THAT'S NOT TRUE. WE'VE GOTTA LEAVE THIS PLACE, SWEET-HEART.

FIND A NEW HOME. QUICKLY!! PUT ON YOUR COAT WHILE I PACK UP. MAKE SURE WE BRING YOUR MEDICINE!

NOW, EMILY!

7

BUT WHY, DADDY?

OH, DAAAADDY. DON'T TALK SILLY.

JUST DO AS YOU'RE TOLD, EMILY!! I-I...

I'M SORRY, SWEETHEART.

I'M SORRY FOR ALL THIS MESS. I'M SORRY FOR YELLING AT YOU. I'M SORRY FOR BEING SUCH A LOUSY FATHER. FOR TRYING TO BE BETTER THAN I AM...

...JUST ANOTHER LUG-HEADED BUM.

I REMEMBER FROM MY CHILDHOOD, THE SOUNDS OF MY FATHER'S RESTLESS PACING AT NIGHT. HE ONCE TOLD ME HOW MY MOTHER USED TO SLEEP LIKE THE DEAD.

IMMEDIATELY REGRETTING HIS CHOICE OF WORDS.

THE NIGHT HAS NEVER HELD PEACE FOR ME.

KNOCK--
KNOCK--
KNOCK--

WELL NOW, MISS BELMONT. I MIGHT ALMOST SAY I'M SURPRISED.

ALMOST.

GOOD EVENING, HUMPHRIES.

HE HERE?

B

SORRY TO SAY, NO. MR. DODDS HAD PRESSING BUSINESS THIS EVENING.

MMM... I SUSPECTED AS MUCH. WHA--?

WHY, SIR! I...I--I DIDN'T HEAR YOU COME IN!

NGUH... I NEE--OH! HELLO, DIAN!

YES, HUMPHRIES, I JUST CAME IN THROUGH THE BACK WAY.

THAT'S FUNNY.

I JUST ARRIVED IN A CAB AND I DIDN'T SEE YOUR CAR PULL IN BEHIND US.

OH. WELL...WE MUST'VE JUST MISSED EACH OTHER.

BUT, HAPPILY... NOT ALTOGETHER.

YES, I'M GLAD.

BUT YOU LOOK RATHER TIRED. PERHAPS I SHOULDN'T STAY...?

NONSENSE. I'M NEVER TOO TIRED FOR ONE OF OUR SPECIAL GAB SESSIONS.

WOULD YOU LIKE SOME TEA?

NO THANKS.

⑨

SO, DIAN...

NN-GHHH...

WH-WHAT'S ON THAT TENACIOUS MIND OF YOURS THIS EVENING?

WES?!

ARE...ARE YOU ALL RIGHT?

FINE. I'M FINE. JUST A BIT OF INDIGESTION.

I, UH...I HAD A CURRY FOR DINNER. I SHOULD KNOW BETTER.

BUT WHAT'S UP WITH YOU? MORE DIRT ABOUT ARTHUR REISLING?

NO, NOTHING SO EXCITING. THIS IS... WELL, I WENT TO A MOVIE WITH MY FRIEND CAROL THIS EVENING. AND AFTERWARDS--RIGHT OUTSIDE THE THEATER--THERE WAS A WOMAN BEATING HER CHILD.

HOW OLD WAS THE CHILD?

A BOY OF ABOUT SEVEN.

⑩

THE THING WAS, NO ONE TRIED TO INTERCEDE. I MEAN, THERE WAS A WHOLE CROWD OF PEOPLE MILLING ABOUT AND THEY ALL JUST ACTED AS IF NOTHING WERE WRONG.

HORRIBLE.

WHEN I WAS GROWING UP IN THE FAR EAST, SUCH SCENES WERE COMMON. I ONCE SAW A VENDOR BREAK HIS SON'S ARM FOR GIVING THE WRONG CHANGE TO A CUSTOMER. NO ONE EVEN BLINKED.

WELL, FINALLY, I COULDN'T TAKE IT ANYMORE AND SO I--I STEPPED INTO THE FRAY. NEARLY HAD TO FIGHT THE WOMAN OFF, MYSELF...

GOOD FOR YOU, DIAN. BRAVO.

SO YOU DON'T THINK I WAS OUT OF LINE? THAT I OVERSTEPPED...

OF COURSE NOT.

THE WORLD WOULD BE A BETTER PLACE IF MORE PEOPLE SPOKE UP WHEN THEY WITNESS INJUSTICE.

:sigh:

SOME DAY I'LL FIGURE OUT JUST WHERE MY HEAD MEETS MY HEART AND THEN YOU WON'T BE PESTERED BY ALL MY SILLY CONFUSIONS.

GOD F--UNNGH! GOD FORBID.

GOODNIGHT, WES. TAKE A BROMO AND GET SOME REST.

CALL ME SOON?

BET ON IT!

NNGHH...

BUT NOT ON MY "HEART-BURNED" RIBS!

11

EXCELLENT, FRANCESCO.

YES, TOMORROW EVENING ON MY YACHT.

I'M ANXIOUS TO DISCUSS THIS VENTURE MORE FULLY WITH YOU. MM-HMM...YES.

UNTIL THE SNOW FALLS, THEN...

GOODBYE.

YES, WHAT *IS* IT, DENNIS?

YOU MAKE ME ILL WITH YOUR CONSTANT PACING.

I JUST HEARD FROM MURPHY. RAMSEY GOT AWAY-- AFTER TALKING TO THE POLICE.

OUR... *FAIL-SAFE* PLAN DIDN'T WORK.

MURPHY CLAIMS RAMSEY HAD SOME MASKED COMPANION. LEVELLED THE BRUTE WITH SOME SORT OF KNOCKOUT GAS.

DISTRESSING. WELL, I SUPPOSE THERE'S NO ALTERNATIVE BUT TO TREAT MR. RAMSEY TO A MORE FINAL SOLUTION.

I THOUGHT AS MUCH.

AND ANY FAMILY THE BASTARD MIGHT HAVE, DENNIS.

DADDY!!

DADDY, I CAUGHT A FROG IN THE GARDEN BUT TOBY KILLED IT WITH A STICK!

DADDY!!

FATHER!

FATHER, I'M HUNGRY! I WANT MY LUNCH NOW!!

⑫

BOYS...

HUNGRY!

I WANNA DRAW!

DENNIS, I'M LATE FOR A MEETING.

TAKE THE BOYS TO THE KITCHEN AND SEE THAT THEY GET SOME LUNCH.

RIGHTO, DAD.

'BYE, FATHER! GOOD-BYE--

NNGPHH--!

HEEEY!

YOU... SHITHEAD!

WHAT?!

YOU PUSHED ME!!

DID TOO!

DID NOT!

BOYS WILL BE BOYS.

OH, YES...

AS THE DREAM FALLS OVER AND THROUGH ME...

...SNOW DRIFTS ACROSS A BLEAK AND DIRTY WORLD. BLANKETING. SOOTHING. MESMERIZING.

UNTIL A BLIZZARD BEGINS TO FORM. OBLITERATING ALL. EVEN THE VOID-THAT-IS-A-MAN...

I CAN SEE NOTHING.

EXCEPT THE CHILDREN. STRUGGLING AGAINST THE INEVITABLE. TRAPPED BY A WORLD GONE MAD WITH DESIRES.

THEIR TEAR-STAINED EYES ARE HOLLOW, CARVED BY TRAGEDY AND FEAR.

I WATCH AS THEY DROWN IN THE SOLID WATERS OF INDIFFERENCE.

THEIR FUTURES SILENCED BY NEGLECT.

THEIR INNOCENCE TRAMPLED...

...BY GREED. 14

SHIT!

LOOKS LIKE WE MISSED 'EM, MURPH.

DAMMIT!!
I KNEW WE SHOULD'A COME LAST NIGHT! GODDAMMIT!!

I TELL YA, DAT BIG BITCH IS MORE TROUBLE... SEARCH IT.

LEFT A LOT O' STUFF. DEY WUZ IN A RUSH.

I GOT A PAIR O' LITTLE GIRL'S PANTIES, ER, I MEAN ...

AN' HERE'S AN ORPHAN ANNIE RING.

NO WOMEN'S STUFF, THOUGH.

ALL RIGHT, LET'S BEAT IT. AT LEAST WE KNOW WHAT WE'RE LOOKIN' FOR NOW.

HE'S GOT A KID WIT' HIM. THAT SHOULD MAKE THINGS EASIER.

15

YOU DOIN' OKAY, SWEETHEART?

JUST A LITTLE COLD, DADDY. IS OUR NEW HOME MUCH FURTHER? I'M REALLY HUNGRY, TOO.

I HOPE SO, BABY. THERE'S ANOTHER PLACE I HEARD ABOUT THAT'S ONLY A FEW BLOCKS FROM HERE.

I'M SORRY, SWEETHEART. THE MAN WANTED TOO MUCH MONEY JUST TO EVEN MOVE IN. WE-- WE'VE GOT TO KEEP LOOKING.

MY TOES FEEL LIKE THEY'RE ON FIRE, DADDY. AND MY TUMMY'S REALLY HUNGRY NOW.

WHERE ARE WE GOING, NEXT?

I...I DON'T KNOW, BABY. DO YOU WANT TO WEAR MY JACKET?

NO, I'LL BE OKA-- HACK! KOFF-KOFF-KOFF! HACK! HACK! HACK! KOFF!

HACK! HACK! KOFF!

HERE, BABY, SIT DOWN. WRAP YOUR-SELF IN THIS.

HACK! HACK! KOFF-KOFF-KOFF!

16

147

Y'LITTLE GIRL'S A LUNGER, EH?

UMM... YEAH. BUT DON'T WORRY, WE WAS JUST MOVIN' ON.

NAH. HAD A SISTER DIED O' THAT. AWFUL COLD OUT FOR SOMEONE WITH THE TB, THOUGH.

WE...WERE EVICTED FROM OUR BUILDING.

GODDAMN BASTARD LANDLORDS.

NEVER MET ONE OF 'EM WASN'T THE MOST COLD-HEARTED SCUM-SUCKERS ON EARTH.

THAT'S TOO BAD, BROTHER.

WHAT'S YOUR NAME, LITTLE LADY?

EM-:KOFF!:... EMILY RAMSEY. AND MY FATHER'S NAME IS CHARLES.

WELL, PLEASED TO MEET YOU BOTH. I'M WILBUR SCHENCK.

I'VE GOT AN ABANDONED SHACK NOT FAR FROM HERE THAT I BEEN SQUATTIN'IN.

IT AIN'T MUCH, BUT YOU'RE WELCOME TO SHARE IT. LEAST KEEP YEZ OUTTA THIS WIND.

WELLLL... I DON'T KNOW, MR. SCHENCK. THAT'S VERY KIND, BUT WE...

HACK! KOFF! KOFF!

PLEASE, DADDY? JUST FOR A LITTLE WHILE?! KOFF-KOFF-KOFF! JUST UNTIL MY HANDS GET WARM?

OKAY, MR. SCHENCK. AND THANK YOU.

NOT NECESSARY, BROTHER. ENJOY THE COMPANY I WILL.

17

WELCOME, MY FRIEND! WELCOME ABOARD THE *LADY KILLER!* I'M SO DELIGHTED TO SEE YOU AGAIN!

MY PLEASURE, MR. REISLING.

MY FATHER SENDS HIS REGARDS AND HOPES THAT WE CAN COME TO AN UNDERSTANDING IN THIS MATTER AS SOON AS POSSIBLE.

OF COURSE, FRANCESCO! OF COURSE. WE ARE, AFTER ALL, MEN OF ACTION, NO?

SO, EXACTLY HOW MUCH HEROIN DO YOU HAVE AVAILABLE?

FORTY-FIVE KILOS.

YOURS FOR TWO-HUNDRED THOUSAND.

A SIZABLE FIGURE -- IN ALL RESPECTS.

(18)

INDEED.

BUT YOU INSISTED ON QUALITY, AND THIS IS PURE AS SILK FROM THE VIRGIN'S VEIL.

MARVELOUS, MY FRIEND. MARVELOUS.

I FIND YOUR PRICE QUITE AGREEABLE. IT SEEMS WE'VE MADE A DEAL!

BUONO.

STILL, MY FATHER HAS INSTRUCTED ME TO ASK... WE HANDLE ALL THE NIGGER TRADE AND THE SPICS. CHINATOWN HAS ITS OWN TRAFFIC.

TELL ME, MR. REISLING, WHERE DO YOU INTEND TO MOVE THIS STUFF? WHO IS YOUR MARKETPLACE?

A MARKET AS YET UNTAPPED BY YOUR FAMILIES, MY FRIEND.

LET'S JUST SAY THAT I HAVE FRIENDS ON THE COAST.

19

DADDY, WHAT DO YOU KNOW ABOUT CHARITY ORGANIZATIONS FOR CHILDREN?

I'M... INTERESTED.

I KNOW THERE ARE SEVERAL, DIAN, WHY DO YOU ASK?

ACTUALLY, THE PERSON TO ASK IS JUDGE SCHAEFFER. HE WAS HIGHLY ACTIVE IN THE JUVENILE COURT SYSTEM FOR A WHILE. IN FACT, I BELIEVE I DO HAVE SOME PHONE NUMBERS IN MY DEN.

I'LL FETCH THEM.

WHAT BROUGHT THIS ON?

OH, CALL IT A WHIM... BUT ONE I'M CONSIDERING SERIOUSLY.

DADDY...?

DIDN'T YOU HEAR ME?

I SAID-- ≈GASP≈

20

YOU, AGAIN.

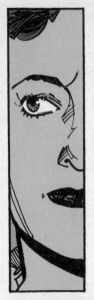

...OR DESTROYED.

IT IS THE FACE OF CORRUPTION THAT ONCE AGAIN BRINGS ME TO YOUR HOME, DISTRICT ATTORNEY. A RIVER OF FILTH THAT WILL NOT LET ME REST UNTIL IT IS DAMMED...

BUT I WOULD PREFER SPEAKING TO YOU IN PRIVATE-- WITHOUT THE ATTENTION OF YOUR DAUGHTER.

YES, OF COURSE.

DIAN, DARLING, WAIT IN THE FRONT ROOM FOR ME. I-I'LL BE FINE, HERE.

AND MAKE NO ATTEMPT TO CONTACT THE POLICE AS YET EITHER, MISS BELMONT.

NOW THEN, UMM... SANDMAN.

I KNOW THAT YOU ARE CURRENTLY INVESTIGATING VARIOUS ALLEGATIONS AGAINST ARTHUR REISLING. HE IS A CLEVER AND HEARTLESS MAN--THE TYPE THAT USUALLY AVOIDS CAPTURE.

BUT NONE CAN ESCAPE THE SANDMAN'S DARK DREAM.

21

YES, WE'VE HEARD RUMORS THAT HE'S INVOLVED IN UNLICENSED BOXING...GLADIATORIAL BOUTS.

ILLEGAL FIGHTING IS ONLY THE TIP OF HIS BLACK ICEBERG.

HIS MEN HAVE TWICE ATTEMPTED TO KILL YOUR INFORMER, CHARLES RAMSEY.

HOW DID YOU KNO--

AND HE IS CURRENTLY ARRANGING WITH THE GAMBONI FAMILY TO DISTRIBUTE A LARGE QUANTITY OF HEROIN.

GOOD LORD! THE GAMBONIS...

REISLING'S MEN BRING WITH THEM AN ENFORCER--A BRUTE OF IMMENSE SIZE AND STRENGTH.

TELL YOUR MEN TO BEWARE. I HAVE ALREADY FELT THE FORCE OF ITS WRATH.

I WILL CONTACT YOU AGAIN WHEN I LEARN MORE OF THIS TRANSACTION.

WE'LL BE READY.

GOODBYE, MR. SANDMAN-- FOR NOW.

AND THANK YOU.

22

HEY, YOU KIDS!! STOP KICKIN' THAT GODDAMN CAN AROUND!!

NYAAHH!!

G'WAN, Y'OLD BAG!!

HA-HA! HA-HA-HA!

K-TANG!

EEYUUW! WHAT STINKS?!

K-TANG

LOOK, STEVIE!! LOOK!

YYYAAAGH!!

NNNGGGH...?

K-TANG!

UNGH.

YOU GODDAMN FOOL!

23

LOOK, I'M SORRY! I ONLY STOPPED FOR A SECOND-- JUST TO BUY A PAPER, FER CHRIS- SAKE!

CAN'T HAVE GOTTEN FAR!

LOOK! OVER THERE! I TOLD YA!!

RECOGNIZE THAT STENCH ANYWHERE!

CLOSE ENOUGH, YOU FOOL! STOP!

TWEEEEE

UNGGH...?

RRMPH.

EASY, SWEETHEART. THAT'S IT. EASY DOES IT.

DC

VERTIGO

NO. 11
FEB 94
$1.95 US
$2.50 CAN
£1.25 UK

SUGGESTED
FOR MATURE
READERS

MATT WAGNER

SANDMAN MYSTERY THEATRE

R. G. TAYLOR

the **BRUTE**

3 of 4

"...felt his bones dance with each blow and then shatter, the slimy meat shoved out of place."

GAVIN WILSON •
RICHARD BRUNING

THE THING THAT HAD FIRST IMPRESSED ME ABOUT DIAN WAS HER STRONGLY DEVELOPED SENSE OF SELF.

WHAT ULTIMATELY CAPTIVATED ME WAS HER GRADUALLY GROWING SENSE OF OTHERS.

HELLOOO, JUDGE SCHAEFFER! OVER HERE!

HELLO, MY DEAR! WHAT A PLEASANT SURPRISE TO HEAR FROM YOU!

YOU HAD MENTIONED THAT YOU NEEDED MY ADVICE?

WELL, DADDY RECOMMENDED I SPEAK TO YOU. AS YOU KNOW, EVER SINCE GRADUATING I'VE BEEN A TRIFLE...LACKADAISICAL.

BUT, TO SOME DEGREE, HE'S RIGHT. I HAVEN'T BEEN ABLE TO FOCUS MY ATTENTION IN ANY ONE DIRECTION AND YET I DO WANT TO MAKE SOMETHING OF MY LIFE.

POOH. THAT'S YOUR FATHER TALKING.

SOMETHING WORTHWHILE.

ANYWAY, I'VE TAKEN AN INTEREST IN THE WELFARE OF UNWANTED CHILDREN. FATHER HAD SAID YOU MIGHT KNOW THE VARIOUS ORGANIZATIONS INVOLVED.

WELL, MOST ASSUREDLY! I BELONG TO SEVERAL SUCH CHARITIES.

SADLY, THERE'S STILL A NEED FOR MANY MORE.

TELL ME, JUDGE, WHY *IS* THERE SO MUCH OF THIS CONDITION?

DON'T PEOPLE *LOVE* THEIR CHILDREN? HOW COULD ANYONE INJURE THEIR OWN SON OR DAUGHTER?

FAR TOO EASILY IT WOULD SEEM, MY DEAR. THE MYTH OF PARENTAL LOVE BEING INNATE IS JUST THAT -- A MYTH.

I JUST CAN'T IMAGINE... OF COURSE, NONE OF MY FRIENDS ACTUALLY HAS ANY KIDS.

HACKK!! <KOFF, KOFF> HACK, HACK!

GLAD YER BACK, BROTHER. I'M HEADIN' OUT.

THANKS FOR STAYIN' WITH HER, MR. SCHENCK.

HOW YA DOIN', BABY?

N--HACK! HACK! NOT SO GOOD, D-KOFF! KOFF!! DADDY...

IT'S NICE TO BE INSIDE... HACK!! HACK!! B-BUT MY CHEST REALLY HURTS...

HERE, BABY. I KNOW THERE'S NOT MUCH LEFT, BUT I FOUND A JOB TODAY.

TAKE SOME OF YOUR MEDICINE. IT'S ALL RIGHT.

OKAY, DADDY...

2

THAT'S IT.

NOW YOU'LL START TO FEEL BETTER. DON'T WORRY, SWEETHEART. I'LL BUY ANOTHER BOTTLE WITH THE MONEY I MAKE TOMORROW.

THE MEDICINE MAKES ME FEEL SLEEPY, DADDY.

THAT MEANS IT'S WORKING, BABY. YOU GET SOME REST.

I'LL BE RIGHT OUTSIDE IF YOU NEED ANYTHING.

G'NIGHT, EMILY.

I LIKE MR. SCHENCK, DADDY. HE LIKES TO PLAY SILLY GAMES.

I HEARD WHAT Y'TOLD HER IN THERE. YOU REALLY FIND SOME WORK T'DAY?

NO, THERE'S NOTHING AVAILABLE.

NOT EVEN GRUNT LABOR.

BUT I DIDN'T WANT EMILY TO WORRY. I'LL TRY AGAIN IN THE MORNING.

WELL, GOOD LUCK, BROTHER!

THEY SAY THINGS ARE GETTIN' BETTER, SO THEY SAY.

③

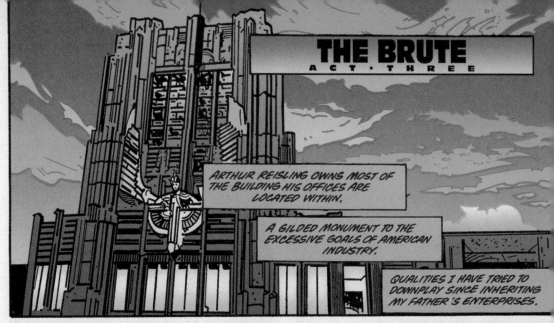

THE BRUTE
ACT · THREE

ARTHUR REISLING OWNS MOST OF THE BUILDING HIS OFFICES ARE LOCATED WITHIN.

A GILDED MONUMENT TO THE EXCESSIVE GOALS OF AMERICAN INDUSTRY.

QUALITIES I HAVE TRIED TO DOWNPLAY SINCE INHERITING MY FATHER'S ENTERPRISES.

YOUR TWO O'CLOCK APPOINTMENT IS HERE, SIR. MR. WESLEY DODDS?

AH YES, MISS BARNES. EXCELLENT, EXCELLENT. SHOW HIM IN!

SHOW HIM IN!

YES, SIR.

NO NEED FOR THAT.

I THINK I COULD HEAR YOUR INVITATION ON THE NEXT STREET, ARTHUR.

HA! HA! QUITE SO...

IT PAYS TO HAVE A COMMANDING VOICE, MY FRIEND! PEOPLE LISTEN WHEN THEY THINK YOU WON'T TAKE NO FOR AN ANSWER!

MMM. I SUPPOSE SO.

SO THEN, GIVEN ANY FURTHER THOUGHT TO MY PROPOSAL?

A BIT.

BUT I WANTED TO THANK YOU FOR THOSE FIGHT TICKETS YOU GAVE TO MY FRIEND, JUDGE SCHAEFFER. HE SAID HE HAD A MARVELOUS TIME.

4

I'M SORRY I HAD TO MISS IT, BUT BUSINESS COMES FIRST. BESIDES, I MUST CONFESS I FIND PROFESSIONAL BOXING A TRIFLE TAME FOR MY TASTES.

HMMM. YOU DON'T SAY...?

YES. WHERE I GREW UP THERE WAS MORE, SHALL WE SAY, FULL-BLOODED BOUTS TO BE SEEN, YOU KNOW...

NO GLOVES AND SUCH.

WELL, I MUST SAY THIS IS A SURPRISE! IT SEEMS I MIGHT BE ABLE TO HELP YOU OUT AS WELL, MY FRIEND.

I SOMETIMES HAVE ACCESS TO MORE... VIGOROUS MATCHES.

WELL!

I WOULD CERTAINLY BE INTERESTED IN ATTENDING SUCH AN EXHIBITION, SIR. MAYBE EVEN AT THE COST OF MY DONATION TO YOUR ANTARCTIC VENTURE.

MARVELOUS! I'M NOT EXACTLY SURE OF WHEN SAID EVENT WOULD TAKE PLACE, BUT I'LL HAVE MY SECRETARY CONTACT YOU AT ONCE.

VERY GOOD.

YOU'VE PUT AN EXCITED SPRING IN MY STRIDE, ARTHUR. I CAN'T WAIT...

WONDERFUL, MY FRIEND. I LOOK FORWARD TO SEEING YOU THEN.

YESSSS, DENNIS?

WE NEED TO TALK, FATHER.

⑤

161

YESSSSS...

SOMETHING MUST BE DONE ABOUT MARIA. THE SITUATION IS GETTING HARDER AND HARDER TO CONTROL.

YOU BOTHER ME ABOUT THAT HERE?! HAVEN'T I GOT ENOUGH OTHER CONCERNS RIGHT NOW?

YOUR "CONCERNS" HAVE ALWAYS BEEN FOR IMMEDIATE GRATIFICATION.

WHICH IS HOW YOU ENDED UP WITH THIS PROBLEM IN THE FIRST PLACE.

WHY... YOU... LITTLE...

...BASTARD! DON'T YOU EVER USE THAT TONE OF VOICE WITH ME.

KRAK

WITHOUT ME, YOU'RE NOTHING! A WEAKLING AND A DRUNK! NOW, GET OUT!

WE'LL SPEAK OF THIS LATER-- AT HOME.

V-VERY WELL, FATHER...

MAY I HELP YOU, SIR?

UMM?!

OH! NO, THANK YOU...

UH.., I...FORGOT MY HAT AND JUST CAME BACK TO RETRIEVE IT. THANK YOU, ANYWAY.

WEIRDO.

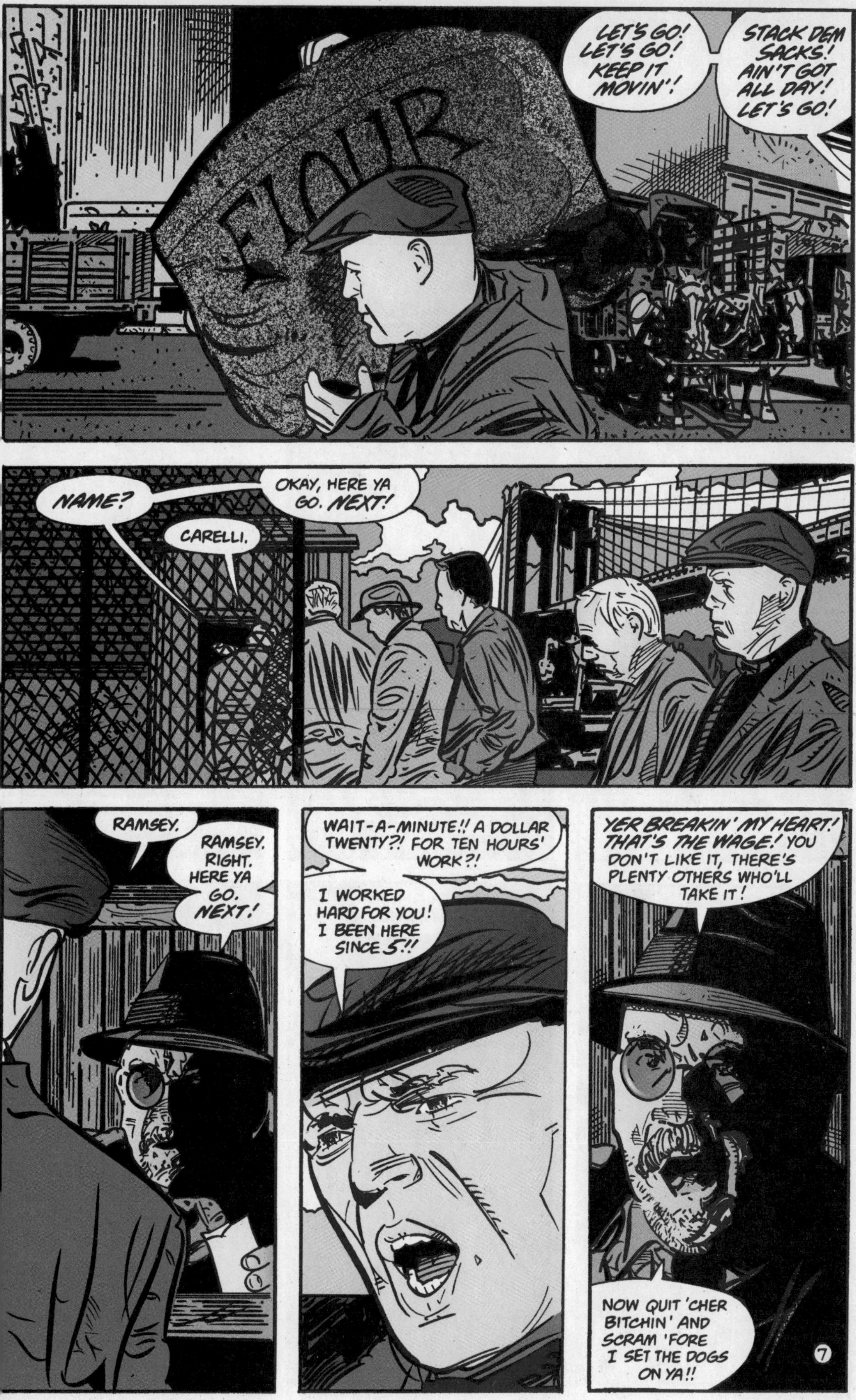

LET'S GO! LET'S GO! KEEP IT MOVIN'!
STACK DEM SACKS! AIN'T GOT ALL DAY! LET'S GO!
FLOUR
NAME?
CARELLI.
OKAY, HERE YA GO. NEXT!
RAMSEY.
RAMSEY. RIGHT. HERE YA GO. NEXT!
WAIT-A-MINUTE!! A DOLLAR TWENTY?! FOR TEN HOURS' WORK?!
I WORKED HARD FOR YOU! I BEEN HERE SINCE 5!!
YER BREAKIN' MY HEART! THAT'S THE WAGE! YOU DON'T LIKE IT, THERE'S PLENTY OTHERS WHO'LL TAKE IT!
NOW QUIT 'CHER BITCHIN' AND SCRAM 'FORE I SET THE DOGS ON YA!!
7

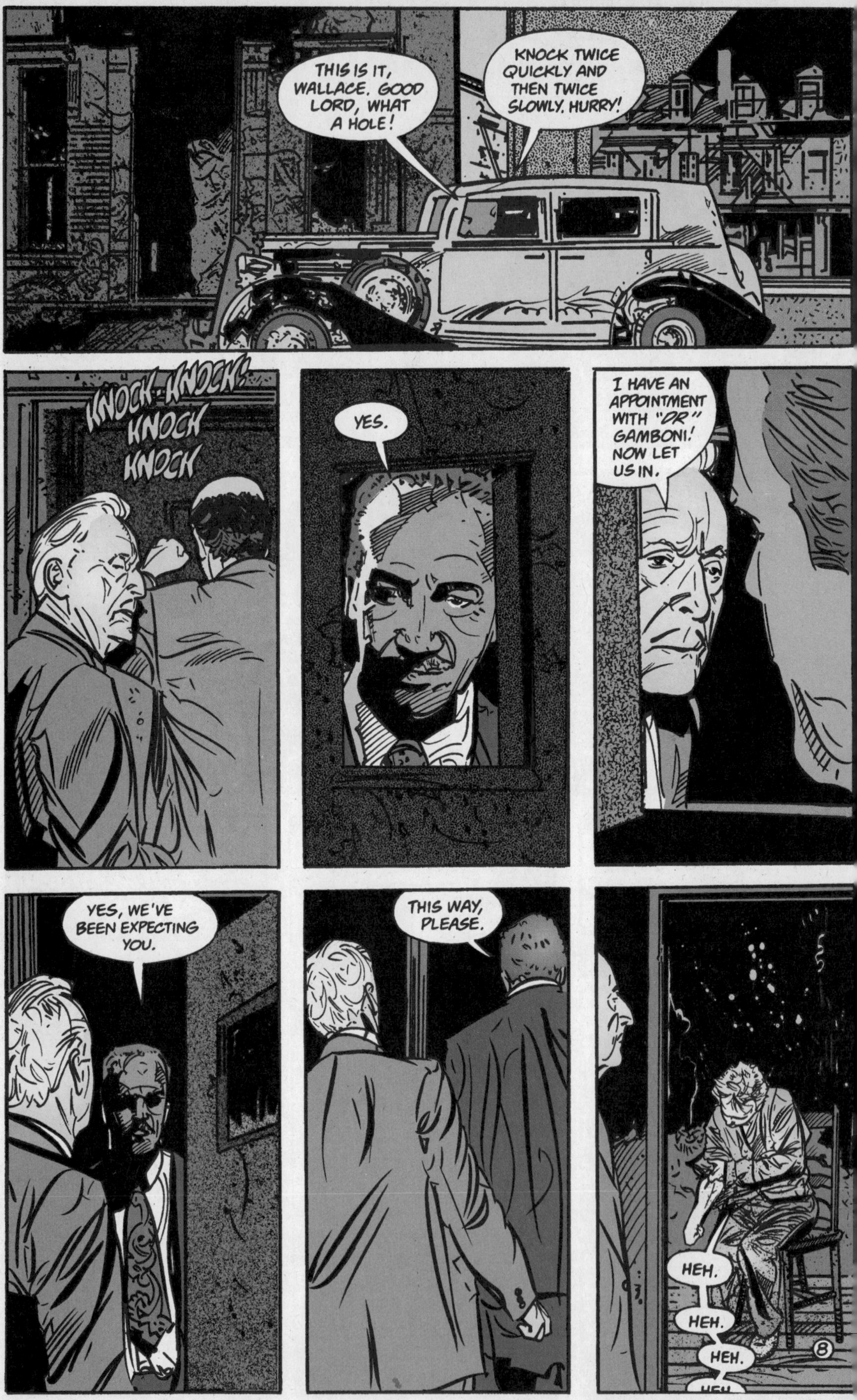
THIS IS IT, WALLACE. GOOD LORD, WHAT A HOLE!
KNOCK TWICE QUICKLY AND THEN TWICE SLOWLY. HURRY!
KNOCK KNOCK! KNOCK KNOCK
YES.
I HAVE AN APPOINTMENT WITH "DR" GAMBONI! NOW LET US IN.
YES, WE'VE BEEN EXPECTING YOU.
THIS WAY, PLEASE.
HEH.
HEH.
HEH.
8

GOOD EVENING TO YOU, MR. REISLING.

MY FATHER SENDS HIS REGARDS.

YES, OF COURSE, FRANCESCO. AND I *APPRECIATE* THE FACT THAT YOU AGREED TO THIS MEETING ON SUCH SHORT NOTICE. STILL, I HADN'T COUNTED ON HAVING TO COME ALL THE WAY UP TO HARLEM.

THESE JUNGLE BUNNIES LIVE LIKE ANIMALS.

IT'S IN THEIR NATURE.

NOW, WHY DID YOU ASK TO SEE ME AGAIN?

YES. WELL, I'M AFRAID I NEED TO EXTEND THE INTENDED DATE OF OUR TRANSACTION JUST A BIT.

IT WAS YOU WHO CAME TO US REQUESTING THIS DEAL IN THE FIRST PLACE.

WE ARE NOT IN THE HABIT OF SITTING ON THE MERCHANDISE FOR SO LONG.

I UNDERSTAND.

BUT AS YOU MUST REALIZE, THE FINANCING OF SUCH A LARGE AMOUNT OF CASH IS... COMPLEX. EVEN FOR ME.

GO ON.

WELL, I JUST NEED A FEW MORE DAYS-- CERTAINLY NO MORE THAN A WEEK.

9

I WILL FORFEIT HALF THE AGREED UPON PRICE IF I AM NOT READY TO PROCEED THEN.

VERY WELL, SIR.

GUARANTEE...?

I GUARANTEE THIS WILL BE RESOLVED WITHIN A WEEK.

AND THEN...?

AND I WISH YOU LUCK AT "SECURING" THE OTHER HALF.

GYM

N° 135

SHOULDN'T OUGHTA BE COMIN' ROUND HERE, RAMSEY.

I JUST WANNA SEE MEL FOR A BIT, GEORGIE.

WELL, WELL, WELL...

IF IT AIN'T THE "ROCKET" HISSELF-- A ROCKET WITH NOWHERE TO LAND!

HIYA, MEL.

Y-GOT A LOTTA GODDAMN BALLS SHOWIN' YER FACE ROUND HERE! I HAD TWO FIGHTS LINED UP FOR YOU THIS WEEK AND YA MISSED 'EM BOTH!

I KNOW, MEL. I KNOW.

I BEEN-- I HAD SOME FAMILY TROUBLE, I'M SORRY.

⑩

BUT NOW I'M BACK.

AND I WANNA FIGHT. PLEASE, MEL. I NEED A BIG PURSE AND I'M *ITCHIN'* TO MIX IT UP. CAN YOU LINE SOMETHIN' QUICK UP FOR ME?

CHRIST, YOU KILL ME.

I CAN'T GET NOTHIN' FOR YOU THIS WEEK, THIS YEAR. MAYBE EVEN THIS *CENTURY!* THE WORD'S OUT ON YOUR CHARLIE-BOY. *"FAMILY TROUBLE"* MY ASSHOLE! I KNOW WHERE YOU BEEN ALL THIS TIME!

RUNNIN' HORSE FOR THE MOB TO THEM NIGGERS UPTOWN!

WH-AAAAT?!

THAT'S A DIRTY LIE! WHO THE HELL TOLD YOU THAT?

UNGH-- WHY, YOU LITTLE...

GET YER GODDAMN MITTS OFFA ME!!

THE WORD'S COME DOWN FROM ABOVE! EVERYBODY KNOWS AND THERE AIN'T *NOTHIN'* I CAN DO TO HELP SAVE YOUR WORTHLESS BUTT!

FACE IT, RAMSEY. YER A LOSER.

TOO BIG, DUMB AND SLOW TO EVEN KNOW WHEN YOU'RE THROUGH. NOW, AMSCRAY--YOU DOPE!

11

YEAH.

I'VE HEARD ABOUT THESE. WORD GETS AROUND.

HOW MUCH AGAIN?

FIVE HUNDRED, AND THAT'S IF YOU LOSE. WINNER TAKES A THOUSAND. IT'S A LOT OF MONEY, BUT THAT'S TO COMPENSATE THE TIME YOU'LL LOSE OUT OF THE REGULAR RING.

SOME MEN TAKE A LITTLE LONGER TO HEAL FROM THESE BOUTS. BESIDES... I KNOW YOU'LL EARN THE MONEY.

I'LL EARN THE THOUSAND.

YOU'RE ON. I'M IN.

EX-CELLENT.

YOU'LL RECEIVE WORD LATER OF WHEN AND WHERE THE FIGHT WILL TAKE PLACE. AND CONGRATULATIONS... YOU OBVIOUSLY HAVE THE SOUL OF A WINNER!

12

ALL RIGHT, ALL RIGHT, EVERYBODY, HEADS UP! WHO'S HUNGRY IN THIS SHACK?

DID YOU BUY US DINNER WITH YOUR JOB MONEY, DADDY?

ALWAYS.

SURE DID, SWEETIE.

I GOT SOME CANNED SOUP, SOME CRACKERS AND EVEN SOME APPLES.

IT'S NOT MUCH, I KNOW...

LOOKS GOOD TO ME. THANK 'Y, BROTHER.

JUST RETURNIN' THE FAVOR.

HERE, EMILY, HAVE SOME SOUP. I'M SORRY IT'S NOT HOT.

IT'S OKAY, DADDY. YUM!

KOFF. KOFF. KOFF.

DADDY, WHEN ARE YOU GOING TO TRY AND FIGHT AGAIN?

YES, PAPA. WHAT ELSE COULD I DO? I GAVE HIM THE WEEK. NO, THAT'S FINE. I'LL CATCH A TAXI.

¡ FWEEET! ¡

HEY, CABBIE! OVER HEAH!

MAMA LEONE'S AND STEP ON IT.

I AM NOT IN A PATIENT MOOD!

MY APOLOGIES, THEN...

PLEASANT DREAMS.

FOOSH!

WHY IS ARTHUR REISLING INVOLVING HIMSELF WITH THE DRUG TRAFFIC?

DUNNO.

PAPA'S BEEN TRYIN' TO FIGURE OUT HIS ANGLE, BUT WE GOT NUTHIN' YET.

WHAT ABOUT THE WEST COAST?

WE CHECKED.

HE GOT NO CONNECTIONS TO THE REGULAR OUTLETS. GO FIGURE.

AND YOU TO SLEEP, MR. GAMBONI.

ZZZZ

14

THE NEXT MORNING FOUND ME ANSWERING A REQUEST TO VISIT DIAN AT HOME. HER DESIRES, I MUST ADMIT, ARE BECOMING QUITE UNDENIABLE.

WELCOME, WESLEY DODDS. I'M SO GLAD YOU COULD COME! I WAS WATCHING FOR YOU FROM THE WINDOW.

MY, OH MY! AND WHAT'S GOT YOU SO EXCITED TODAY?

SURELY NOT JUST A VISIT FROM ME?

WELL...NOT COMPLETELY. YOU REMEMBER THE INCIDENT WITH THE BOY AND HIS MOTHER?

ABSOLUTELY.

WELL, I'VE BEEN THINKING A LOT ABOUT THAT AND SO JUDGE SCHAEFFER HAS HELPED ME GET IN TOUCH WITH SOME CHILDREN'S CHARITIES.

OH, REALLY?

MMM... THE UNITED WAY.

THEY SAID I HAD NO EXPERIENCE AT FIELD WORK BUT COULD CERTAINLY CANVASS FOR DONATIONS. SO, I WAS WONDERING...

SAY NO MORE! HOW'S THREE-HUNDRED SOUND?

WONDERFUL! WELL, NOW *THAT* WAS CERTAINLY EASY!

WELL, I SHOULD THINK IT'S A POPULAR CAUSE. I MUST BE GOING NOW, BUT KEEP AT IT, DIAN.

HOW MANY WEALTHY PEOPLE DO YOU KNOW?

OH, ENOUGH... I SUPPOSE. THANKS, WES.

YOU'VE JUST GIVEN ME A GREAT IDEA AS WELL.

15

RING RING

REISLING RESIDENCE.

HELLO? YES, I'M CALLING FOR ARTHUR REISLING ON BEHALF OF THE UNITED WAY. MY NAME IS DIAN BELMONT AND I MET MR. REISLING RECENTLY AT--

ONE MOMENT, PLEASE. I'LL SEE IF HE'S IN.

ARTHUR REISLING. YES, MISS BELMONT, OF COURSE I REMEMBER. YOU WERE WESLEY DODDS'S LOVELY COMPANION.

TELL ME, MISS BELMONT. HOW DID YOU GET MY HOME NUMBER?

OH THAT. I'VE DONE SOME LEGAL CLERKING. IT'S NOT REALLY THAT HARD TO FIND UN-LISTED NUMBERS IF ONE KNOWS HOW.

I SEE. WELL THEN, YOUNG LADY, WHAT CAN I DO FOR YOU?

IT'S NOT FOR ME. YOU SEE, I'VE JUST STARTED WORKING WITH THE UNITED WAY AND I'D LIKE TO SEE IF YOU WERE INTERESTED IN DONATING...

VERY INTERESTED. BUT I'M ALL TIED UP FOR THE REST OF THIS WEEK. SHALL WE MEET NEXT MONDAY? HERE. AT, SAY...ONE O'CLOCK?

WHY, YES, THAT WOULD BE FINE...

DELIGHTFUL. UNTIL THEN, MISS BELMONT.

16

IT WAS LATER IN THE WEEK THAT I RECEIVED WORD FROM ARTHUR REISLING OF AN EVENING OF "SOPHISTICATED ENTERTAINMENT" AT HIS ESTATE.

LESS THAN THREE DAYS AFTER HANDING OVER MONEY FOR THE BENEFIT OF CHILDREN, I WAS HERE TO WATCH GROWN MEN PUMMEL EACH OTHER SENSELESSLY.

THE DRIVEWAY AND LAWN WERE PARKED FULL OF LIMOUSINES.

MR. WESLEY DODDS, SIR.

DODDS!! GOOD SHOW, OLD MAN! SO VERY GLAD YOU COULD COME!

THANKS TO YOUR GENEROUS INVITATION, ARTHUR.

17

BARTLEY SAYS THEY'RE READY FOR MORE HORS D'OEUVRES UP FRONT.

MM-HMM... I GOT EM. DEY ALMOST READY.

I'LL SAY ONE THING 'BOUT RICH FOLKS. THEY SURE GO FOR SOMETHIN' THAT'S FREE.

WHY, YOU'D THINK THEY WAS ALL HALF-STARVIN'!

DO YOU HOST THESE EVENTS REGULARLY?

MMM. WE TRY TO STAGE A BOUT EVERY QUARTER OR SO. OTHERWISE I DON'T THINK THIS OLD BALL-ROOM WOULD SEE ANY USE.

YOU'LL EXCUSE ME FOR A MOMENT?

GOOD EVENING, FINE PATRONS OF PUGILISM!

I'D LIKE TO WELCOME YOU ALL TO ANOTHER EVENING OF PASSION-ATE DISTRACTION.

18

AND NOW, SEEING AS HOW BOTH OUR FIGHTERS HAVE ENTERED THE RING, LET THE FESTIVITIES BEGIN!

DING-DING

THE ACTION BEGAN LIKE A NORMAL BOUT, BUT THE ATMOSPHERE WAS DIFFERENT.

THE FIGHTERS WERE VISIBLY PAINED BY EACH AND EVERY CONNECTION.

AND THE CROWD WAS DEATHLY SILENT.

EACH BLOW BECAME AN EXPLOSION. EACH GRUNT A CACOPHONY.

HOW CAN SOMEONE WILLINGLY SUBJECT THEMSELVES TO THIS?

DING DING!

: pant-pant-pant :

NOW COMES THE GOOD PART, DODDS!

UMMM... YES, SO I SEE. GOODY.

DING-DING!

NNUNGH--

YOU GOTTA LOTTA BALLS, ASSHOLE.

MMPH!

BUT Y' BRAINS ARE KINDA SOFT!

20

UUNMPH--

PRACK!

HIS... JAW...

EXCUSE ME, ARTHUR. I HATE TO DO THIS, BUT...

CAN YOU DIRECT ME TO THE REST ROOM?

MMM...?

OH. UH, YES... THERE'S ONE BY THE ENTRANCE TO THE GARDEN. ON YOUR RIGHT.

THANK YOU, ARTHUR. SORRY ABOUT THIS. ALWAYS DID HAVE THE SMALLEST BLADDER...

DAMN INCONVENIENT.

SORRY.

HE'S OVER HERE, MURPH! BY THE PATIO WALL.

WELL, WELL, HELLO AGAIN, ASSHOLE.

COME TO VISIT US AGAIN, HUH?

YOU MISS US THAT MUCH, HUH?

NAHHH...

HE JUST LIKES WATCHIN' PEOPLE GET THRASHED!

I CAN UNDERSTAND THAT.

TWEEEE

21

NNNUGHH...?

OH, NO...

PLEASE, FELLAS...

DON'T...

THAAAAT'S IT. LET'S HAVE A LITTLE BEGGIN'.

ALWAYS MAKES THINGS A LITTLE SWEETER!

NO! NOOOOO!!

NOT SO LOUD, SHITHEAD!

CHCK!

GO FOR IT, BABY!

NNNGHH!

SPAK!

SPAK! SPAK!

YAAA

SPAK!

AAAA

AAA

:GASP!:

OH...TH-THANK GOD F-FOR... NIGHT AIR!

:GULP:

HUH... HUH... HUH...

EH?

MAN, OH MAN, HE FLEW OUTTA HERE LIKE A BAT OUTTA HELL!!

YEAH, HEH-HEH, BUT A BAT WITH ONLY ONE WING!

HA! HA! HA! HA! HA!

C'MON, Y'BIG BRUTE! THIS WAY!

NNGHH!

NNGHH!

NNGHH!

NNH--EM... EMILY!!

OH, SWEET JESUS, MARY AND JOSEPH.

EMILY...?!

BABY?!

WHERE ARE YOU?!

HERE, DADDY...

M'OVERHERE, DADDY...

23

179

EMILY...?

EMILY, ARE YOU ALL RIGHT?

YOUR DRESS! YOU'RE...

...BLEEDING?!

BUT--BUT YOU'RE NOT OLD ENOUGH...

IT HURTS, DADDY.

I'M TRYING TO BE GOOD.

BE BRAVE.

IT'S OKAY, BABY. WHAT HURTS?

BUT IT HURTS!!

THE NEW MEDICINE HURTS, DADDY!

IT HURTS ME DOWN WHERE I PEE!

BUT, SWEETHEART, I DIDN'T BUY ANY...

MR. SCHENCK'S MEDICINE!

HE SAID...

HE SAID IT WOULD HELP ME NOT COUGH.

I TOLD HIM I DIDN'T WANT HIS MEDICINE!

BUT HE WOULDN'T STOP DOING IT! HE SAID IT...

WH--WHAT DID HE DO, EMILY...?

HE PUT THE MEDICINE IN DOWN WHERE I PEE.

HE PUT IT IN WITH HIS DADDY-THING AND IT HURT.

I TOLD HIM I DIDN'T WANT ANY MEDICINE!

BUT HE WOULDN'T STOP DOING IT...

OH...OH NO, EMILY!

OH NO, MY BABY!!

OH NO!

NO!

NOOOOOO!

"...as blood gathered around her like spiders. The screaming had suddenly stopped."
MATT WAGNER
SANDMAN MYSTERY THEATRE
R.G.TAYLOR
GAVIN WILSON • RICHARD BRUNING

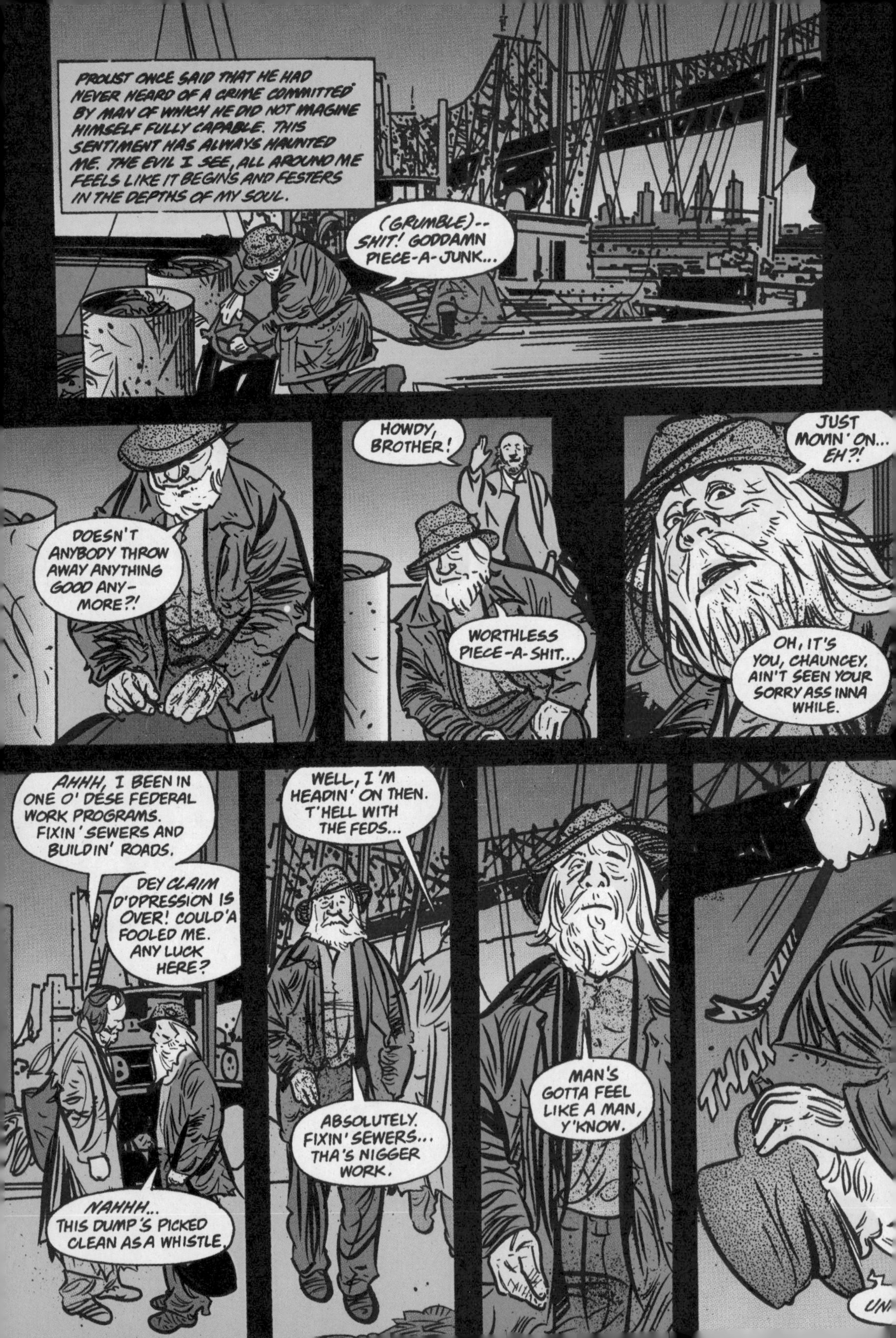
PROUST ONCE SAID THAT HE HAD NEVER HEARD OF A CRIME COMMITTED BY MAN OF WHICH HE DID NOT IMAGINE HIMSELF FULLY CAPABLE. THIS SENTIMENT HAS ALWAYS HAUNTED ME. THE EVIL I SEE, ALL AROUND ME FEELS LIKE IT BEGINS AND FESTERS IN THE DEPTHS OF MY SOUL.
(GRUMBLE)-- SHIT! GODDAMN PIECE-A-JUNK...
DOESN'T ANYBODY THROW AWAY ANYTHING GOOD ANY-MORE?!
HOWDY, BROTHER!
WORTHLESS PIECE-A-SHIT...
JUST MOVIN' ON... EH?!
OH, IT'S YOU, CHAUNCEY. AIN'T SEEN YOUR SORRY ASS INNA WHILE.
AHHH, I BEEN IN ONE O' DESE FEDERAL WORK PROGRAMS. FIXIN' SEWERS AND BUILDIN' ROADS.
DEY CLAIM D'DPRESSION IS OVER! COULD'A FOOLED ME. ANY LUCK HERE?
NAHHH... THIS DUMP'S PICKED CLEAN AS A WHISTLE.
WELL, I'M HEADIN' ON THEN. T'HELL WITH THE FEDS...
ABSOLUTELY. FIXIN' SEWERS... THA'S NIGGER WORK.
MAN'S GOTTA FEEL LIKE A MAN, Y'KNOW.
THAK

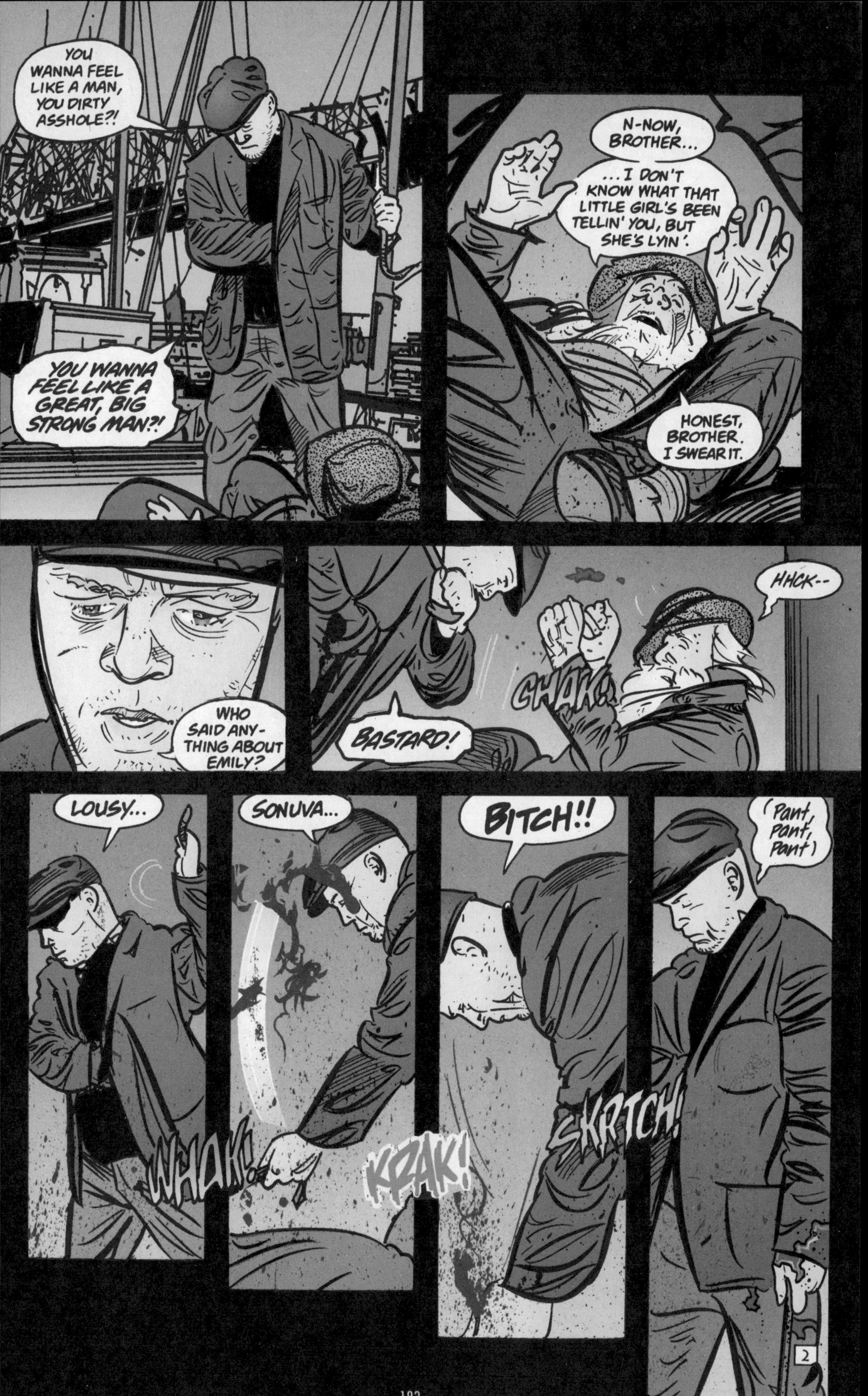

YOU WANNA FEEL LIKE A MAN, YOU DIRTY ASSHOLE?!
YOU WANNA FEEL LIKE A GREAT, BIG STRONG MAN?!
N-NOW, BROTHER...
...I DON'T KNOW WHAT THAT LITTLE GIRL'S BEEN TELLIN' YOU, BUT SHE'S LYIN'.
HONEST, BROTHER. I SWEAR IT.
WHO SAID ANY-THING ABOUT EMILY?
HHCK--
CHAK!
BASTARD!
LOUSY...
WHAK!
SONUVA...
KRAK!
BITCH!!
SKRTCH!
(Pant, pant, Pant)
2

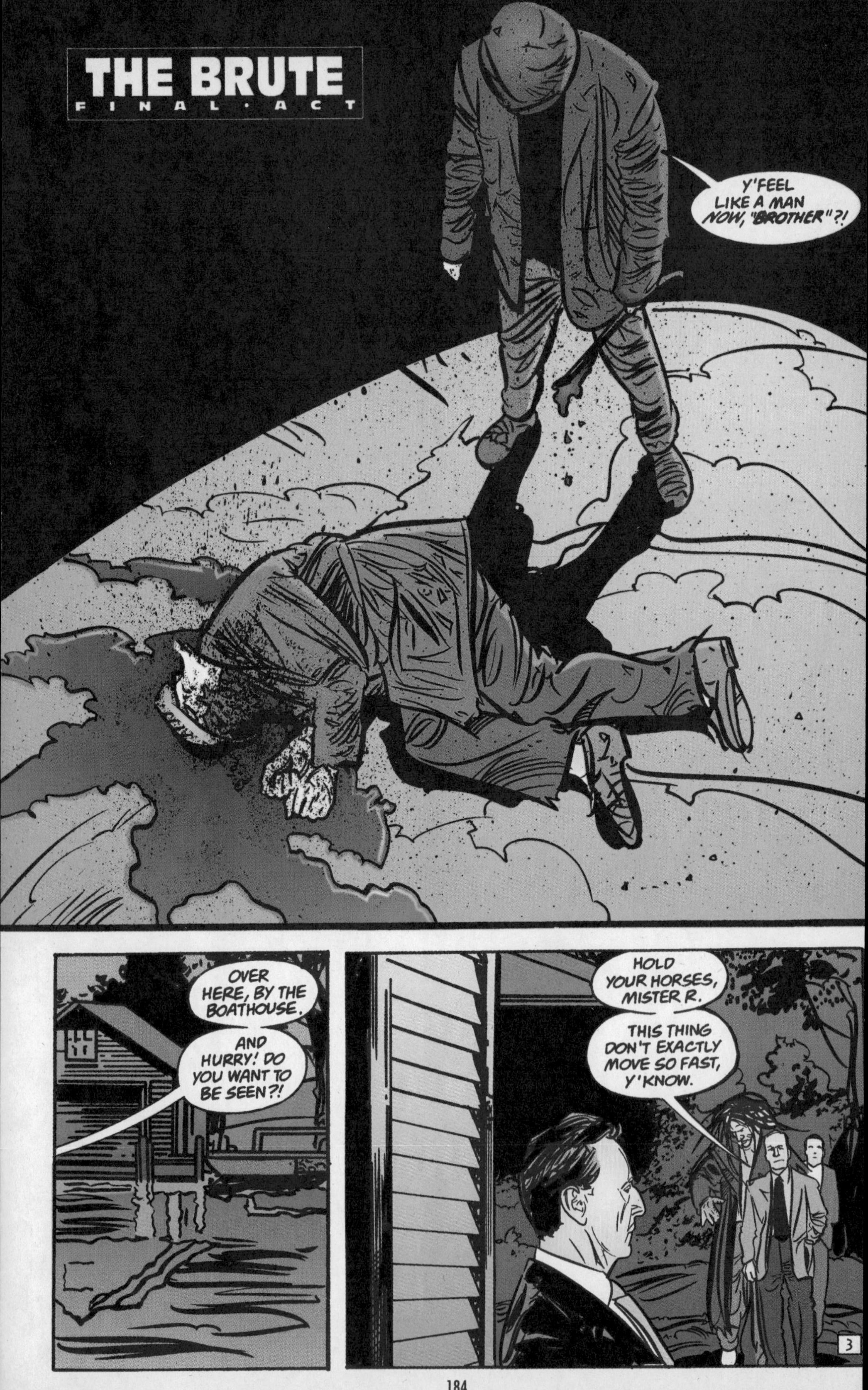
THE BRUTE
FINAL·ACT
Y'FEEL LIKE A MAN NOW, "BROTHER"?!
OVER HERE, BY THE BOATHOUSE.
AND HURRY! DO YOU WANT TO BE SEEN?!
HOLD YOUR HORSES, MISTER R.
THIS THING DON'T EXACTLY MOVE SO FAST, Y'KNOW.
3

THAT'LL BE ENOUGH OF THAT TALK! THIS *PERSON* IS NOT A "*THING*"

THERE YOU GO, DARLING. INSIDE. THAT'S IT.

THAT WILL BE ALL, "*GENTLEMEN.*"

YEAH, YEAH. SORRY IF WE HURT THE "*PERSON'S*" FEELINGS.

C'MON, LET'S PEEK IN ON THE FIGHT.

HERE. YOU *MUST* EAT SOMETHING.

BE CAREFUL! IT'S VERY WARM!

NNNGH...

THAT'S A DARLING. VERY GOOD.

AND HERE'S YOUR FAVORITE DOLL, SWEETHEART.

DON'T KNOW WHAT BECAME OF THE HEAD.

N-NNMMM... PHT-PHT...

4

MY FATHER TRIED TO RUN AWAY FROM THE EVIL INSIDE HIM. I, IN TURN, STRUGGLE TO DEFEAT IT.

THE BIG EVENT'S ALL DONE WITH, HUH? WELL, THANKS FOR AN... INVIGORATING EVENING, ARTHUR.

CERTAINLY, DODDS! I'M SORRY YOU HAD TO MISS SO MUCH OF IT.

OH, THAT'S ALL RIGHT. MY OWN FAULT.

I'LL HAVE MY ACCOUNTANT SEND YOU THE EXPEDITION FUNDS TOMORROW.

AND THANKS AGAIN. GOOD NIGHT.

ANYTIME, DODDS. ANYTIME...

THE SAD REALITY IS THAT I OFTEN SLUMBER THROUGH SOME OF THE MOST GLARING AGGRESSIONS. EVIL NEVER SLEEPS.

TAXI

WHA--? WHY, MR. REISLING! I'M SURPRISED TO SEE YOU ANSWERING THE DOOR YOURSELF.

MOST OF THE SERVANTS HAVE THE DAY OFF, MY DEAR.

BUT, COME IN! COME IN! LOVELY TO SEE YOU AGAIN. LOVELIER THAN LAST TIME AS WELL, I MIGHT ADD.

WELL... THANK YOU, SIR.

PLEASE, MAKE IT ARTHUR.

BUT, FIRST... LET'S SETTLE INTO SOME PLACE MORE COMFORTABLE, SHALL WE?

VERY WELL, I...

I'VE ASKED THE COOK TO BRING US TEA IN MY PRIVATE STUDY.

5

THANK YOU, MARTHA. THAT WILL BE ALL FOR NOW.

EXCELLENT.

NOW, THEN...

CL-CLICK!

WE HAVE A WONDERFUL OPPORTUNITY TO GET TO *KNOW* ONE ANOTHER BETTER...

DON'T WE?

WELL, YES, I...

ER, THAT IS...

YOUR HOUSE IS VERY IMPRESSIVE, MR. REISLING. *UH*...ARTHUR.

YES, WELL, MOST THINGS ABOUT ME *ARE* SO, MY DEAR. WOULD YOU...

...CARE TO SEE MORE?

OH! WELL... MAYBE SOME OTHER TIME...

WHAT I CAME HERE FOR IS TO SPEAK ABOUT *THE UNITED WAY*...

AH, YES... YOUR CHARITY WORK. SUCH A *WARM* PERSON YOU ARE.

YES, AND A TRIFLE *TOO* WARM AT THE MOMENT, THANK YOU.

IT'S TO BE THAT WAY, IS IT?

6

TELL ME, THEN...

WHY DID YOU EVEN COME HERE IN THE FIRST PLACE?

I TOLD YOU ON THE PHONE! I'M CANVASSING FOR THE UNITED WAY AND THOUGHT YOU MIGHT--

OH, MALARKEY! YOU WOMEN ALWAYS HAVE TO PUT UP A RESISTANCE AT FIRST.

NOW LEAN BACK. YOUR LEGS ARE VERY SMOOTH.

SIR!

I DID NOT COME HERE TO MAKE MYSELF AVAILABLE TO YOU!

THIS IS BECOMING TIRESOME.

BUT IT DOES MAKE YOUR SKIN FLUSH VERY NICELY.

MR. REISLING, STOP--

COME, COME, MY DEAR. YOU'RE N NUN, I CAN TELL, AN WHY ELSE DOES A WO GO TO A MAN'S HOU UNESCORTED?

MY, YOU DO HAVE SUCH LOVELY FIRM BREASTS.

DON'T TOUCH ME!

WAP

UH...?!

WHY...YOU... LITTLE...

TRAMP!

ACK-- ST-STOP...

YOU'RE JUST THE SAME-- ALL YOU LITTLE BITCH. WHAT YOU NEED.

...IS A GOOD HARD MAN--UCK!

FUD!

AAAHHHH... YOU--YOU-- YOU...

REAP WHAT YOU SOW, MR. REISLING. LET GO!

GODDAMN LITTLE WHORE!

SHOW YOU...

I SAID, LET GO!!

THUN

URF--

THE ONLY THING I NEED FROM YOU, MR. REISLING, IS A RESPECTFUL DISTANCE. I CAN LET MYSELF OUT, THANK YOU.

NNNGGH...

NN... WHORES, HING B--BUT BITCHES AND WHORES... NNNGHH...

TOB-EEEE...

SHHH...

I WANNA SEE, TOO.

SHUT UP, ASS-WIPE.

NO FAIR.

IT'S MY TURN. I WANNA SEE THEM F--

I TOLD YOU TO SHUT UP!

KLUD

OW! NO FAIR.

I DREAM OF MYSELF ON AN INFINITE, DESOLATE PLANE. NOT MYSELF AS I AM...

...BUT AS I WOULD RATHER BE. MORE POWERFUL AND SEVERE. MY SENSE OF JUSTICE LIKE ICE. THE MASK MORE PROTECTIVE AND FRIGHTENING.

ITS OBLIQUE CONTOURS FILTERING OUT THE POISON OF HUMAN EXISTENCE.

ITS GEOGRAPHY, AN ARCTIC PRISON OF MAN'S SINS AND SUFFERINGS.

THE BEASTS OF ETERNAL DAMNATION.

CREATURES WE WOULD HUNT AND ERADICATE WITH OUR SILLY LAWS.

FOR WHEN THE COURTS FLAY OPEN SUCH CARCASSES...

THEY NEVER REVEAL WHAT THEY FIND.

THE AWFUL TRUTH OF IT IS...

MR. DODDS?

WE ARE, ALL OF US, STUCK FAST IN THE ICE.

HMM... HUH? WH-WHAT IS IT, HUMPHRIES?

SORRY TO WAKEN YOU, SIR. BUT, MISS BELMONT IS DOWNSTAIRS AND SHE SEEMS REALLY QUITE UPSET.

DIAN? I'LL BE RIGHT DOWN.

DIAN! SORRY TO KEEP YOU WAITING, BUT YOU CAUGHT ME ASLEEP.

DIAN? DIAN, WHAT IS IT? WHAT'S WRONG?

OHHH, WESLEY, I'M SORRY. I'M SORRY TO ALWAYS COME CRYING TO YOU LIKE THIS...

SHHH...

IT'S JUST THAT ...I--HE...

CALM DOWN. NOW TELL ME WHAT'S HAPPENED.

I--I WENT TO SEE ARTHUR REISLING ABOUT A DONATION TO MY CHARITY.

WELL, I WAS NO SOONER THERE THAN HE LOCKED ME IN HIS STUDY AND MADE A PASS AT ME.

HE WHAT?

AND MORE THAN JUST THAT. HE FONDLED ME. STUCK HIS HAND UP MY SKIRT. I THINK HE WOULD'VE RAPED ME IF I HADN'T GOTTEN AWAY!

WHY, THAT...

THAT... SONUVABITCH!!

10

I KNEW HE WAS CAPABLE OF SOMETHING LIKE THIS! BUT I NEVER DREAMED THAT YOU...

I WAS ABLE TO FEND HIM OFF. BRAINED HIM WITH AN ASHTRAY. BUT THEN... TO BREAK DOWN LIKE THIS AFTERWARDS -- I JUST FEEL SO...

W-WES?

IF ONLY I'D DONE SOMETHING EARLIER. IF ONLY I'D NEVER LET IT COME TO THIS...

WES, PLEASE, IT'S OKAY.

YOU COULDN'T HAVE KNOWN THIS WOULD HAPPEN. I WENT THERE OF MY OWN ACCORD.

I KNOW.

OH, DIAN, I'M SORRY.

WHEN I THINK WHAT MIGHT'VE HAPPENED...

I KNOW, BUT IT'S OKAY.

I'M OKAY. REALLY.

DIAN, I...

11

192

HEY, RAMSEY! I'M HERE.

TULLY! THANKS A LOT FOR MEETIN' ME LIKE THIS.

HEY, YOU WAS ALWAYS A GOOD EGG NO MATTER WHAT ANYBODY SAYS.

SO...THIS YOUR LITTLE GIRL?

YEAH. YEAH, THIS IS HER. SAY HELLO TO MR. TULLY, SWEETHEART.

DON'T WANT ANY MORE MEDICINE, DADDY. NO MORE.

UMM... CUTE KID.

SO...DID YOU GET WHAT I ASKED?

YEAH, YEAH. I GOT IT.

NOTHIN' TO BRAG ABOUT, THOUGH. USED TO BE MY OLD MAN'S TRAPPIN' PIECE. HE USED IT TO TAKE OUT BEAVERS N' SHIT.

ALMOST RUSTED TO HELL, BUT IT SHOULD STILL WORK.

SO...NOW THE BIG QUESTION WHAT IN THE HELL DO YOU NEED A GAT FOR?

FOR--FOR PROTECTION, TULLY. I GOT-- GOTTA PROTECT MY LITTLE GIRL.

SHE'S ALL THAT I GOT NOW.

193

DIAN, I'M SORRY...

YOU CAME HERE FOR COMFORT AND I'M... I'M ACTING LIKE ARTHUR REISLING.

C'MERE, YOU.

AND SHUT UP.

MMMM...

HEH.

BUT, SERIOUSLY NOW, ARE YOU ALL RIGHT, DID HE HURT YOU?

I'M FINE.

REALLY. A TRIFLE SHAKEN BUT OTHERWISE FINE.

DO YOU... WANT TO STAY HERE TONIGHT?

YES. I DO.

BUT I THINK I'D BETTER NOT. I WOULDN'T WANT SUCH A NIGHT TO BE TAINTED BY SUCH A DAY.

BUT I DO WANT TO.

I UNDERSTAND. AND IT'S JUST AS WELL...

I HAVE SOME UNFINISHED BUSINESS TO WRAP UP.

GOOD-NIGHT, WESLEY.

PLEASANT DREAMS, DIAN.

13

NNNGGG...

NGNN...?

YOUR MIND IS THAT OF A CHILD, AND YOUR STRUCTURE THAT OF A MONSTER.

UNGGH... UNG...UNG...

CL-CLICK!

NN-GGAAHH!

PLEASANT DREAMS, GENTLE BRUTE.

BUT TRUE MONSTERS ARE MARKED BY THEIR INTENTIONS.

FOOSH

14

DINNERTIME, SWEETHEART...

WHAT TH--

THOSE *IDIOTS* MUST'VE LEFT THE DOOR UNLOCKED.

(*sniff, sniff*)

GOOD LORD, WHAT IS THAT *SMELL*?!

I-- *OH NO!* WHAT HAVE THEY DONE TO YOU?!

OH, THOSE... THOSE *THUGS!* DID *THEY* TIE YOU UP LIKE THIS?!

BASTARDS!

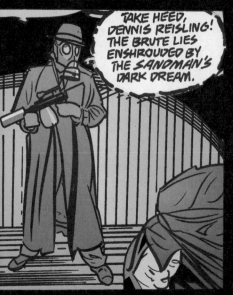

TAKE HEED, *DENNIS REISLING!* THE BRUTE LIES ENSHROUDED BY THE *SANDMAN'S* DARK DREAM.

WHO-- WHO ARE YOU?! AND *WHAT* HAVE YOU DONE TO HER?!

HER...?!

15

YES, HER.

HER NAME IS MARIA. SHE I-- SHE IS MY SISTER.

SHE WAS BORN THUS?

NO. NO, SHE WAS BORN A QUITE NORMAL AND BEAUTIFUL LITTLE GIRL.

HER ONLY PROBLEM WAS BEING BORN ILLEGITIMATE. LIKE ME.

BUT YOUR FATHER IS A WIDOWER.

FROM DOROTHY. A LATER AFFAIR. SHE DIED GIVING BIRTH TO THE TWINS.

MY MOTHER-- OUR MOTHER'S NAME WAS ELIZABETH.

FATHER ALWAYS DID HAVE A CONSUMPTIVE TASTE FOR WOMEN. AND MOTHER WAS REALLY QUITE A SIMPLE GIRL-- WHO BELIEVED ALL HIS PROMISES AND LIES.

SHE NEVER REALLY WANTED THE CHILDREN HE LEFT HER WITH.

I WAS ONLY SIX WHEN HE LEFT TO SEEK HIS FORTUNES ABROAD, PROMISING ALL OF US HE WOULD BE BACK IN A MONTH.

MONTHS TURNED INTO YEARS AS MOTHER'S SANITY CAME AND WENT LIKE THE TIDE.

LIVING AS A SINGLE WOMAN ALONE WITH TWO CHILDREN WAS AN UNBEARABLE CROSS FOR HER.

WHAT HAPPENED TO MARIA?

ONE DAY, MOTHER'S MIND JUST BROKE IN HALF. MARIA HAD BEEN CRYING FOR DAYS. IT --

IT WASN'T HER FAULT. SHE'D HAD A STOMACH FLU AND WAS SOILING HERSELF CONSTANTLY. FINALLY, MOTHER JUST COULDN'T TAKE IT ANYMORE...

SHE LOCKED MARIA IN A SMALL CLOSET BENEATH THE STAIRS. JUST LOCKED HER AWAY -- AS IF SHE DIDN'T EXIST ANYMORE.

M--MARIA STAYED IN THAT CLOSET FOR ALMOST THREE YEARS.

MOTHER REFUSED TO ACKNOWLEDGE THE HORRIBLE SCREAMING AND POUNDING. SHE DIDN'T EVEN SEEM TO NOTICE THE UNBEARABLE STENCH THAT SOON AROSE.

I--I FEARED MY MOTHER'S WRATH BUT COULDN'T TURN AWAY FROM THIS TRAGEDY. I BROUGHT MARIA FOOD AND DID MY BEST TO CLEAN OUT THE MESS IN HER CELL.

BUT THE BABY SISTER I HAD KNOWN WAS NO MORE. SHE BATTERED HERSELF AGAINST THE WALLS AND I ASSUME THIS LED TO HER GROWTH DEFORMITY.

EVENTUALLY, FATHER DID RETURN TO CLAIM US BOTH. MOTHER, HE HAD COMMITTED TO AN ASYLUM. SH-SHE DIED PEACE-FULLY IN HER SLEEP.

BUT MARIA, THE TRUE VICTIM OF HIS GODDAMN INDIFFERENCE... SHE NEVER HAD IT SO LUCKY.

SHE SERVES THE WHIMS OF HIS ARROGANCE NOW, BUT SHE IS REALLY QUITE BLAMELESS...

NONE OF IT WAS EVER REALLY HER FAULT, YOU SEE... NOT HER FAULT AT ALL...

17

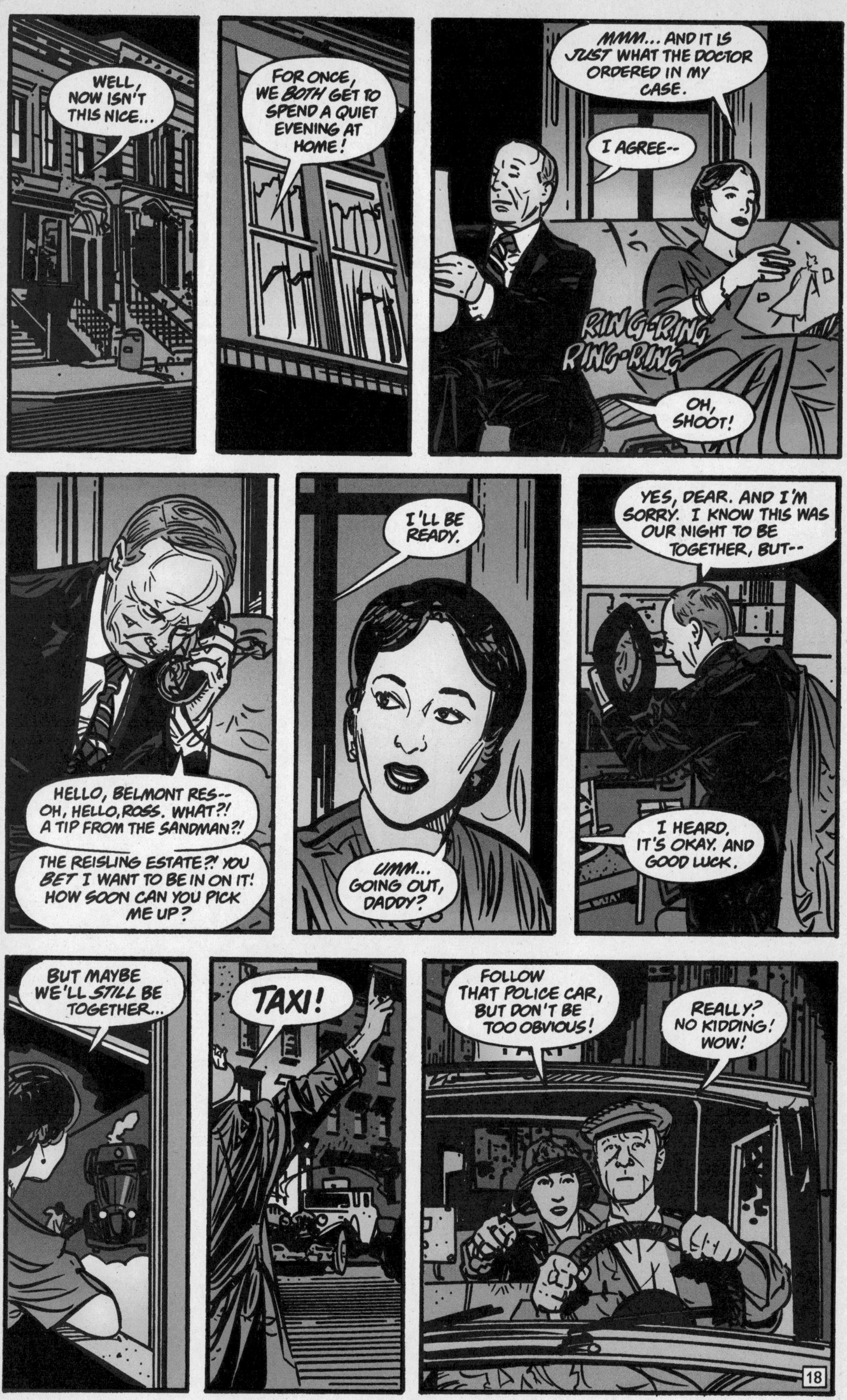

WELL, NOW ISN'T THIS NICE...
FOR ONCE, WE BOTH GET TO SPEND A QUIET EVENING AT HOME!
MMM... AND IT IS JUST WHAT THE DOCTOR ORDERED IN MY CASE.
I AGREE--
RING-RING RING-RING
OH, SHOOT!
HELLO, BELMONT RES-- OH, HELLO, ROSS. WHAT?! A TIP FROM THE SANDMAN?!
THE REISLING ESTATE?! YOU BET I WANT TO BE IN ON IT! HOW SOON CAN YOU PICK ME UP?
I'LL BE READY.
UMM... GOING OUT, DADDY?
YES, DEAR. AND I'M SORRY. I KNOW THIS WAS OUR NIGHT TO BE TOGETHER, BUT--
I HEARD. IT'S OKAY. AND GOOD LUCK.
BUT MAYBE WE'LL STILL BE TOGETHER...
TAXI!
FOLLOW THAT POLICE CAR, BUT DON'T BE TOO OBVIOUS!
REALLY? NO KIDDING! WOW!
18

THEY'RE HERE.

AND DENNIS IS LATE. DAMN HIM!

SHOW OUR GUESTS IN, WALLACE.

YES, SIR.

GOOD EVENING TO YOU, MISTER REISLING.

WELCOME, WELCOME, FRANCESCO. AND TO YOUR "FRIEND."

YOUR MERCHANDISE.

YOU ARE SUCH A BUSINESSMAN, FRANKIE. WALLACE, LAY THE MONEY SATCHEL ON THE TABLE AS WELL.

CARLO, OPEN OUR PACKAGE SO THAT MR. REISLING MAY INSPECT HIS PURCHASE.

SI, FRANCESCO. I--AGGH!!

POW!

OKAY, NOBODY MOVES. YOU GODDAMN SUIT-AND-TIE SLIMEBALLS...

19

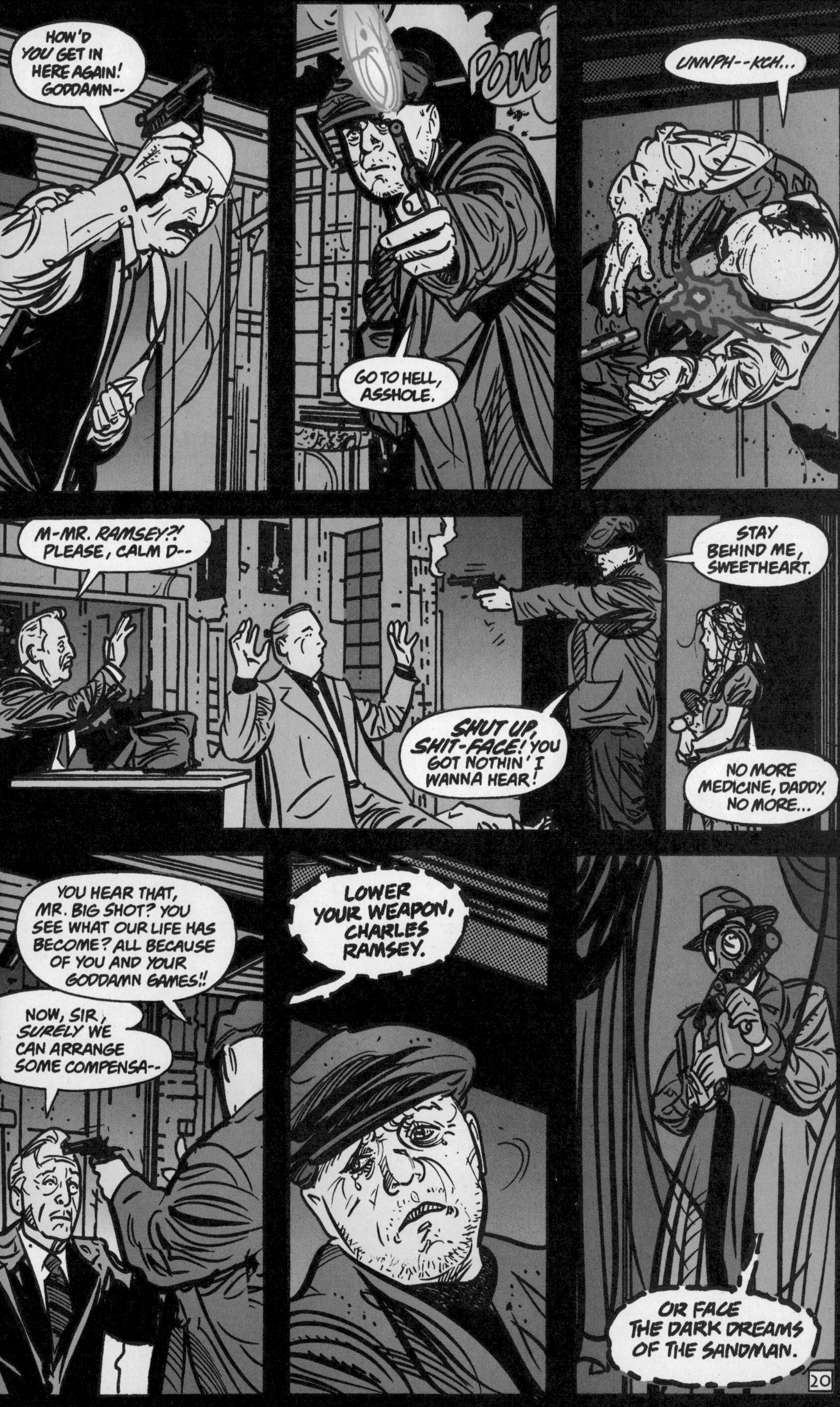
HOW'D YOU GET IN HERE AGAIN! GODDAMN--
POW!
GO TO HELL, ASSHOLE.
UNNPH--KCH...
M-MR. RAMSEY?! PLEASE, CALM D--
SHUT UP, SHIT-FACE! YOU GOT NOTHIN' I WANNA HEAR!
STAY BEHIND ME, SWEETHEART.
NO MORE MEDICINE, DADDY. NO MORE...
YOU HEAR THAT, MR. BIG SHOT? YOU SEE WHAT OUR LIFE HAS BECOME? ALL BECAUSE OF YOU AND YOUR GODDAMN GAMES!!
NOW, SIR, SURELY WE CAN ARRANGE SOME COMPENSA--
LOWER YOUR WEAPON, CHARLES RAMSEY.
OR FACE THE DARK DREAMS OF THE SANDMAN.
20

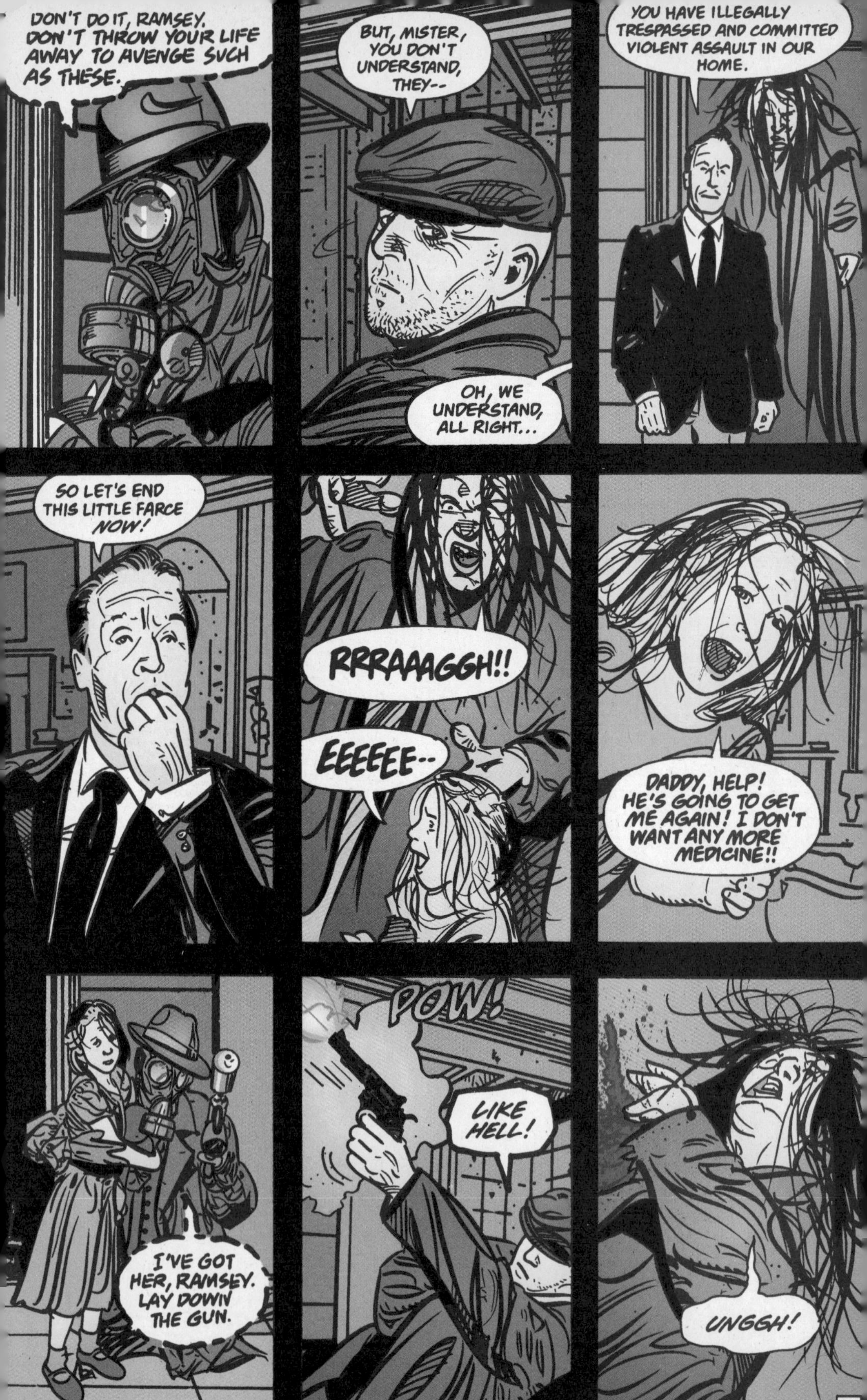
DON'T DO IT, RAMSEY. DON'T THROW YOUR LIFE AWAY TO AVENGE SUCH AS THESE.
BUT, MISTER, YOU DON'T UNDERSTAND, THEY--
OH, WE UNDERSTAND, ALL RIGHT...
YOU HAVE ILLEGALLY TRESPASSED AND COMMITTED VIOLENT ASSAULT IN OUR HOME.
SO LET'S END THIS LITTLE FARCE NOW!
RRRAAAGGH!!
EEEEEE--
DADDY, HELP! HE'S GOING TO GET ME AGAIN! I DON'T WANT ANY MORE MEDICINE!!
I'VE GOT HER, RAMSEY. LAY DOWN THE GUN.
POW!
LIKE HELL!
UNGGH!

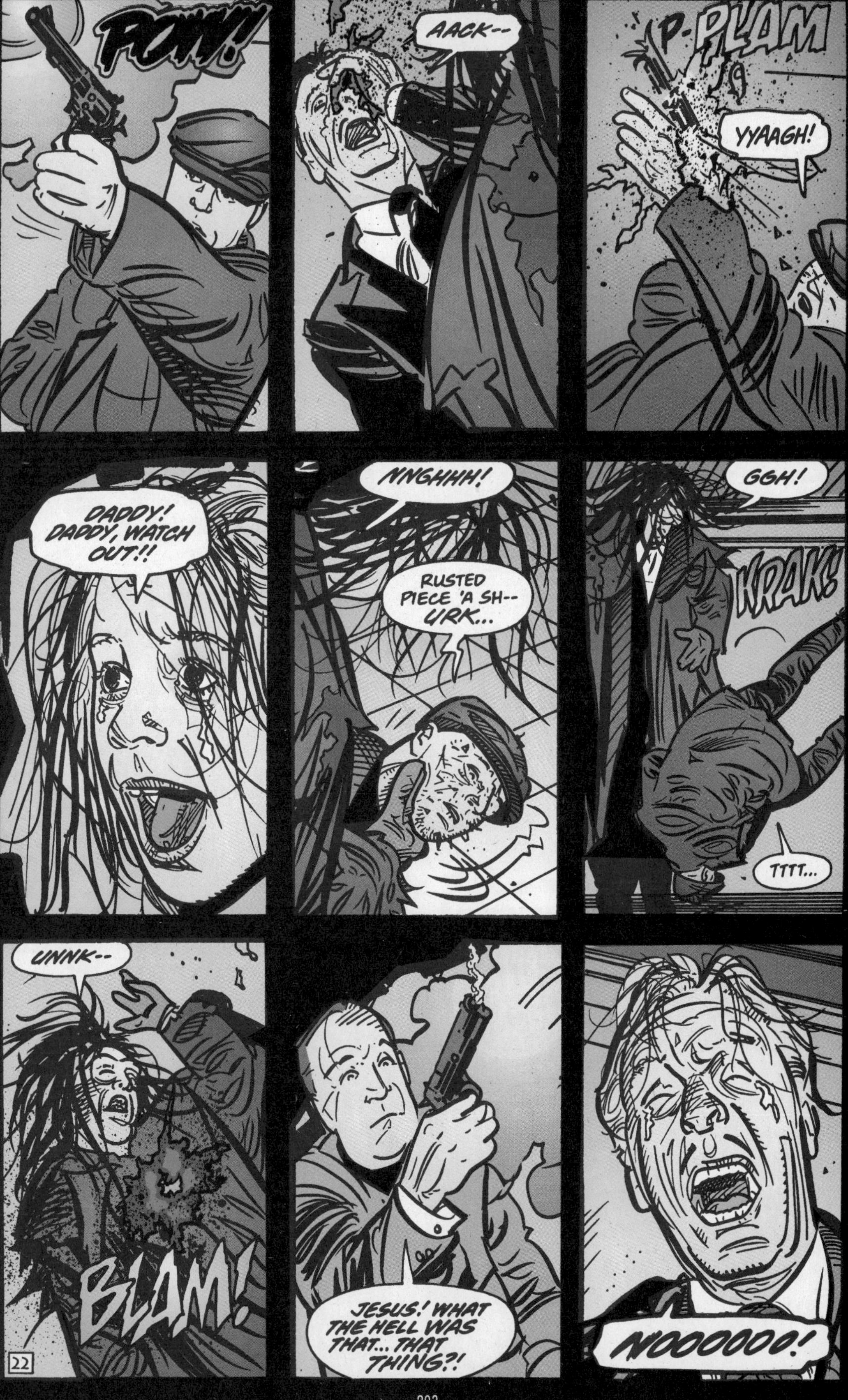
POW!
AACK--
P-PLAM
YYAAGH!
DADDY! DADDY, WATCH OUT!!
NNGHHH!
RUSTED PIECE 'A SH-- URK...
GGH!
KRAK!
TTTT...
UNNK--
BLAM!
22
JESUS! WHAT THE HELL WAS THAT... THAT THING?!
NOOOOOO!

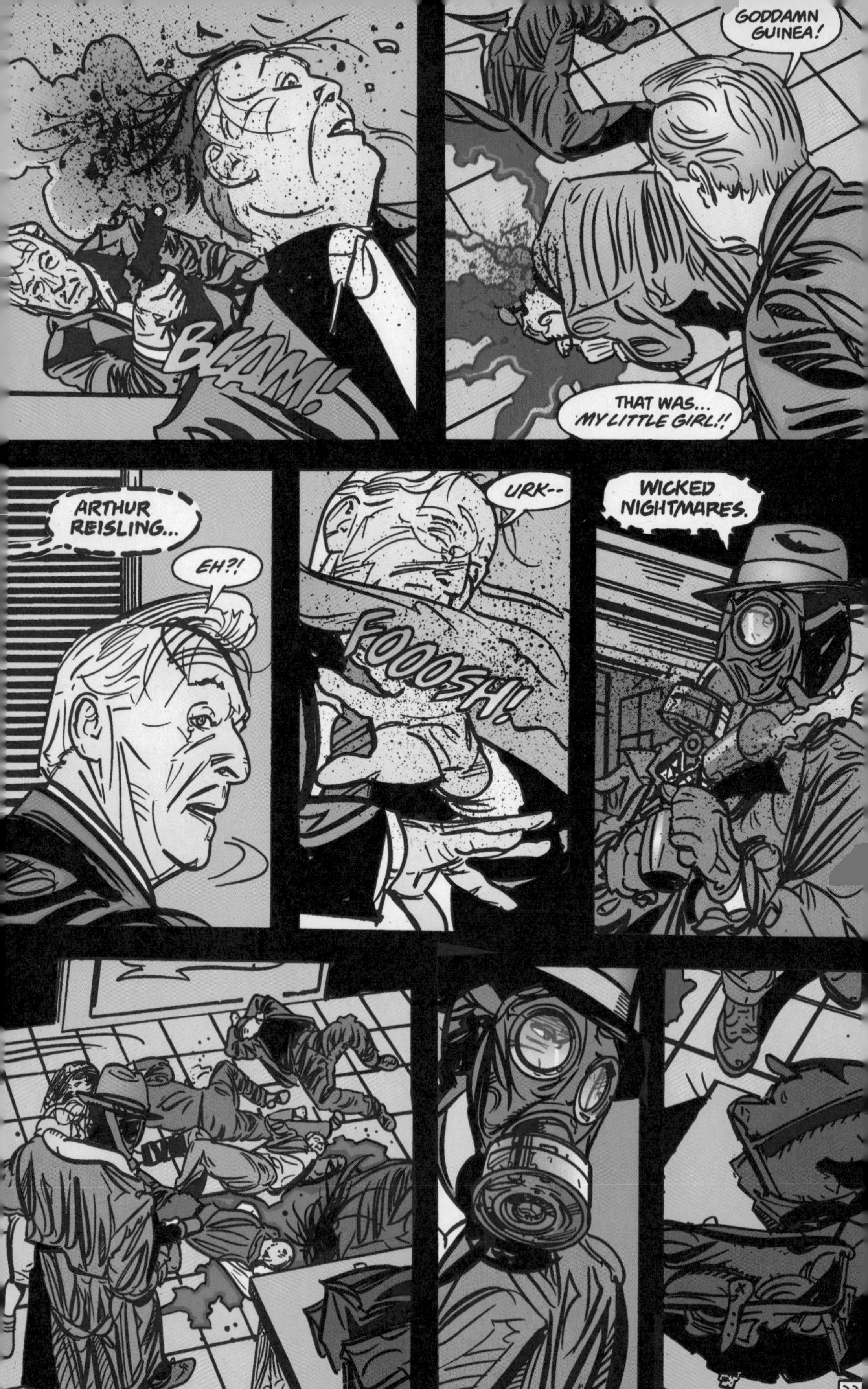
BLAM!
GODDAMN GUINEA!
THAT WAS... MY LITTLE GIRL!!
ARTHUR REISLING...
EH?!
URK--
FOOOSH!
WICKED NIGHTMARES.

THIS IS IT.

CHRIST, LOOK AT ALL THOSE COP CARS!

MUST BE AN' INVASION 'R SOMETHIN'!

BUT THAT'S IT FOR ME, LADY. I AIN'T GETTIN' NO CLOSER. YOU CAN WALK THE REST OF THE WAY. THAT'LL BE THREE BUCKS.

BUT-- ¡TSK¡ OHHH... ALL RIGHT.

GO NO FURTHER TOWARDS THE HOUSE, MISS BELMONT. THEREIN LIES ONLY BLOODSHED AND DEATH.

NO PLACE FOR THE CURIOUS.

YOU?!!

THIS GIRL IS A VICTIM OF THE EVIL WROUGHT INSIDE. PLEASE, SEE THAT SHE FINDS PROPER CARE.

YES. YES, I WILL.

ARE--ARE YOU ALL RIGHT? WERE YOU INJURED IN ANY WAY?

HMM... GUESS HE DIDN'T HEAR ME.

24

SO YOUR "QUIET EVENING AT HOME" TURNED OUT TO BE NOTHING OF THE SORT?

SORRY TO SAY, NO. BUT AT LEAST THERE WAS SOME RESOLUTION TO THIS WHOLE REISLING AFFAIR. HE WON'T BE PEDDLING DRUGS, FIXING FIGHTS OR ACCOSTING WOMEN FOR QUITE SOME TIME TO COME!

DRUGS?

YES. IT SEEMS REISLING WAS ATTEMPTING TO FLOOD SOME WEST COAST UNIVERSITY CAMPUSES WITH HEROIN. SEEMS LIKE A STUPID STUNT. EVEN COLLEGE KIDS AREN'T THAT WILD!

ANYWAY, THEY WERE RIGHT IN THE MIDDLE OF MAKING THIS DEAL WHEN THE SANDMAN BROKE THINGS UP.

YOU SEEM QUITE INTRIGUED WITH THIS CHAP.

WHO, THE SANDMAN?

WELL, LET'S JUST SAY HE'S CERTAINLY OUT OF THE ORDINARY. YOU KNOW THE POLICE FOUND THAT SATCHEL OF HEROIN BURNING IN REISLING'S FIRE-PLACE.

AND I SUPPOSE HE KEPT ALL THE MONEY FROM SUCH A DEAL.

WELL...NOT EXACTLY. YOU SEE, AN ANONYMOUS BENE-FACTOR HAS SET UP A TRUST FUND IN EMILY RAMSEY'S NAME.

THE POLICE CAN'T REALLY PROVE IT'S THE MONEY FROM THAT NIGHT, SOOO...

I SAY, THAT IS FUNNY. WHAT A CLEVER FELLOW!

YES, I THOUGHT YOU'D LIKE THAT.

IN FACT, IT SOUNDS JUST LIKE THE SORT OF UNASSUMING THING YOU MIGHT DO YOURSELF.

(giggle) I CERTAINLY HOPE SO, MR. DODDS!

OH, REALLY? WELL THEN, TELL ME, MISS BELMONT, DOES THIS SEEM LIKE SOME-THING I'D DO?

THE End

R. Taylor

100 BULLETS
Brian Azzarello/Eduardo Risso
With one special briefcase, Agent Graves gives you the chance to kill without retribution. But what is the real price for this chance — and who is setting it?

Vol 1: FIRST SHOT, LAST CALL
Vol 2: SPLIT SECOND CHANCE
Vol 3: HANG UP ON THE HANG LOW
Vol 4: A FOREGONE TOMORROW
Vol 5: THE COUNTERFIFTH DETECTIVE
Vol 6: SIX FEET UNDER THE GUN

AMERICAN CENTURY
**Howard Chaykin/David Tischman/
Marc Laming/John Stokes**
The 1950s were no picnic, but for a sharp operator like Harry Kraft opportunity still knocked all over the world — and usually brought trouble right through the door with it.

Vol 1: SCARS & STRIPES
Vol 2: HOLLYWOOD BABYLON

ANIMAL MAN
**Grant Morrison/Chas Truog/
Doug Hazlewood/various**
A minor super-hero's consciousness is raised higher and higher until he becomes aware of his own fictitious nature in this revolutionary and existential series.

Vol 1: ANIMAL MAN
Vol 2: ORIGIN OF THE SPECIES
Vol 3: DEUS EX MACHINA

THE BOOKS OF MAGIC
Neil Gaiman/various
A quartet of fallen mystics introduce the world of magic to young Tim Hunter, who is destined to become the world's most powerful magician.

THE BOOKS OF MAGIC
John Ney Rieber/Peter Gross/various
The continuing trials and adventures of Tim Hunter, whose magical talents bring extra trouble and confusion to his adolescence.

Vol 1: BINDINGS
Vol 2: SUMMONINGS
Vol 3: RECKONINGS
Vol 4: TRANSFORMATIONS
Vol 5: GIRL IN THE BOX
Vol 6: THE BURNING GIRL
Vol 7: DEATH AFTER DEATH

DEATH: AT DEATH'S DOOR
Jill Thompson
Part fanciful *manga* retelling of the acclaimed THE SANDMAN: SEASON OF MISTS and part original story of the party from Hell.

DEATH: THE HIGH COST OF LIVING
**Neil Gaiman/Chris Bachalo/
Mark Buckingham**
One day every century, Death assumes mortal form to learn more about the lives she must take.

DEATH: THE TIME OF YOUR LIFE
**Neil Gaiman/Chris Bachalo/
Mark Buckingham/Mark Pennington**
A young lesbian mother strikes a deal with Death for the life of her son in a story about fame, relationships, and rock and roll.

FABLES
**Bill Willingham/Mark Buckingham/
Lan Medina/Steve Leialoha/Craig Hamilton**
The immortal characters of popular fairy tales have been driven from their homelands and now live hidden among us, trying to cope with life in 21st-century Manhattan.

Vol 1: LEGENDS IN EXILE
Vol 2: ANIMAL FARM
Vol 3: STORYBOOK LOVE

HELLBLAZER
**Jamie Delano/Garth Ennis/Warren Ellis/
Brian Azzarello/Steve Dillon/
Marcelo Frusin/various**
Where horror, dark magic, and bad luck meet, John Constantine is never far away.

ORIGINAL SINS
DANGEROUS HABITS
FEAR AND LOATHING
TAINTED LOVE
DAMNATION'S FLAME
RAKE AT THE GATES OF HELL
SON OF MAN
HAUNTED
HARD TIME
GOOD INTENTIONS
FREEZES OVER
HIGHWATER

THE INVISIBLES
Grant Morrison/various
The saga of a terrifying conspiracy and the resistance movement combating it — a secret underground of ultra-cool guerrilla cells trained in ontological and physical anarchy.

Vol 1: SAY YOU WANT A REVOLUTION
Vol 2: APOCALIPSTICK
Vol 3: ENTROPY IN THE U.K.
Vol 4: BLOODY HELL IN AMERICA
Vol 5: COUNTING TO NONE
Vol 6: KISSING MR. QUIMPER
Vol 7: THE INVISIBLE KINGDOM

LUCIFER
**Mike Carey/Peter Gross/Scott Hampton/
Chris Weston/Dean Ormston/various**
Walking out of Hell (and out of the pages of THE SANDMAN), an ambitious Lucifer Morningstar creates a new cosmos modeled after his own image.

Vol 1: DEVIL IN THE GATEWAY
Vol 2: CHILDREN AND MONSTERS
Vol 3: A DALLIANCE WITH THE DAMNED
Vol 4: THE DIVINE COMEDY
Vol 5: INFERNO

PREACHER
Garth Ennis/Steve Dillon/various
A modern American epic of life, death, God, love, and redemption — filled with sex, booze, and blood.

Vol 1: GONE TO TEXAS
Vol 2: UNTIL THE END OF THE WORLD
Vol 3: PROUD AMERICANS
Vol 4: ANCIENT HISTORY
Vol 5: DIXIE FRIED
Vol 6: WAR IN THE SUN
Vol 7: SALVATION
Vol 8: ALL HELL'S A-COMING
Vol 9: ALAMO

THE SANDMAN
Neil Gaiman/various
One of the most acclaimed and celebrated comics titles ever published.

Vol 1: PRELUDES & NOCTURNES
Vol 2: THE DOLL'S HOUSE
Vol 3: DREAM COUNTRY
Vol 4: SEASON OF MISTS
Vol 5: A GAME OF YOU

Vol 6: FABLES & REFLECTIONS
Vol 7: BRIEF LIVES
Vol 8: WORLDS' END
Vol 9: THE KINDLY ONES
Vol 10: THE WAKE
Vol 11: ENDLESS NIGHTS

THE SANDMAN: THE DREAM HUNTERS
Neil Gaiman/Yoshitaka Amano
Set in Japan and told in illustrated prose, this adult fairy tale featuring the Lord of Dreams is beautifully painted by legendary artist Yoshitaka Amano.

THE SANDMAN: DUST COVERS —
THE COLLECTED SANDMAN COVERS
1989-1997
Dave McKean/Neil Gaiman
A complete portfolio of Dave McKean's celebrated SANDMAN cover art, together with commentary by McKean and Gaiman.

THE SANDMAN COMPANION
Hy Bender
A dreamer's guide to THE SANDMAN, featuring artwork, essays, analysis, and interviews with Neil Gaiman and many of his collaborators.

THE QUOTABLE SANDMAN
Neil Gaiman/various
A mini-hardcover of memorable quotes from THE SANDMAN accompanied by a host of renditions of Morpheus and the Endless.

SWAMP THING: DARK GENESIS
Len Wein/Berni Wrightson
A gothic nightmare is brought to life with this horrifying yet poignant story of a man transformed into a monster.

SWAMP THING
**Alan Moore/Stephen Bissette/John Totleben/
Rick Veitch/various**
The writer and the series that revolutionized comics — a masterpiece of lyrical fantasy.

Vol 1: SAGA OF THE SWAMP THING
Vol 2: LOVE & DEATH
Vol 3: THE CURSE
Vol 4: A MURDER OF CROWS
Vol 5: EARTH TO EARTH
Vol 6: REUNION

TRANSMETROPOLITAN
Warren Ellis/Darick Robertson/various
An exuberant trip into a frenetic future, where outlaw journalist Spider Jerusalem battles hypocrisy, corruption, and sobriety.

Vol 1: BACK ON THE STREET
Vol 2: LUST FOR LIFE
Vol 3: YEAR OF THE BASTARD
Vol 4: THE NEW SCUM
Vol 5: LONELY CITY
Vol 6: GOUGE AWAY
Vol 7: SPIDER'S THRASH
Vol 8: DIRGE
Vol 9: THE CURE
Vol 10: ONE MORE TIME

Y: THE LAST MAN
**Brian K. Vaughan/Pia Guerra/
José Marzán, Jr.**
An unexplained plague kills every male mammal on Earth — all except Yorick Brown and his pet monkey. Will he survive this new, emasculated world to discover what killed his fellow men?

Vol 1: UNMANNED
Vol 2: CYCLES
Vol 3: ONE SMALL STEP